Menus and Recipes for International & Occasional Cuisines

Charles McDonald

Outskirts Press, Inc.
http://www.outskirtspress.com

ISBN: 978-1-9772-5815-1

Cover Photo © 2023 www.gettyimages.com. All rights reserved - used with permission.

Outskirts Press and the "OP" logo are trademarks belonging to Outskirts Press, Inc.

PRINTED IN THE UNITED STATES OF AMERICA

*Menus with Recipes for International &
Occasional Cuisines*

Chef Charles McDonald

International & Occasional Cuisines

An orphan's journey from Malta to acclaimed American chef.

I dedicate this book to my mother Rita McDonald who was my inspiration into the culinary world.

Acknowledgements:

To my friends who have helped me on the journey of my book's publication.

Stephanie Ursini

Larry Ursini

Mary Jo Long

Dale Brunn

Ryan & Samantha Miller

Kevin & Valerie Trechter

Mark Cesario

Introduction . . .

My book begins with an autobiography detailing my journey to the United States of America from the island of Malta when I was adopted by an American family. I provide a detailed story of the trials, tribulations and triumphs of learning a new culture and language. I also offer a bit of history on places where I started my career in the restaurant business from High School Home Economics to the Navy cooking school and then to the Colorado Culinary Art Institute.

Over the course of my culinary career and now in retirement, cooking has always been my passion. My family, friends, colleagues, and customers refer to me as *Chef Charles* and it is very endearing to me because I have enjoyed every minute of cooking for them all. What I have learned over the years is that I not only enjoy cooking, but I love creating new recipes too. I'm not sure how many I've created to date, but if I had to guess, probably over a thousand! I've had such fun creating recipes for restaurants, large and small events, and fund raisers.

A few years ago, my family and friends gave me the idea to write a book so I could share them with everyone! Unique to my book, different than a typical cookbook of recipes, is that I have created twenty-four, unique menus for occasions such as birthdays, anniversaries, New Year's Day, Valentine's Day as well as diversity menus that include Cinco de Mayo, Gay Pride Day, and Juneteenth just to name a few. They range from four to six delicious courses with step-by-step details for preparation and enjoyment. While I don't feature a picture with each recipe, I feel confident that my instructions will make all the dinners a huge success! Simply select an occasion and have the full menu and recipes at your fingertips and of course feel free to mix and match your favorites.

This book has been a true *Labor of Love* and I hope you enjoy my recipes as much as I have loved putting them together for you.

Bon Appetit . . .

Chef Charles McDonald

Autobiography of Chef Charles McDonald . . .

Born January 10, 1950, with the name of Master Carmel Borg in a small coastal town of Gozo Island, next to the main island of Malta in the Mediterranean Sea. Charles was conceived by his birth mother MaryAnne Borg (his father is unknown). At the age of three months old, Charles's mother turned over her son to a Catholic orphanage on the main island of Malta in the capital town of Valletta where Charles was offered to the Ursuline nuns to be raised in the Catholic orphanage until he was adopted at seven years old.

In 1999, my adopted mother and I went to Malta to see where I was born. These were the only two nuns left that raised me from 3 months old to 7 years old.

GOZO AND COMINO

Gozo is just four miles away to the northwest across a clear blue and very deep channel. The two islands are connected by regular car and passenger ferry and a helicopter service. Gozo is where Odysseus is said to have been held captive entranced by the nymph Calypso. This sister island is almost entirely agricultural, and life is simple but comfortable. It is an island of farmers and fishermen, and their way of life dominates the character of Gozo.

If you arrive by sea, *Mgarr Harbour* is pictur-

Mgarr Harbour

A family from the United States of America in a small town of Pueblo, Colorado, read an article for adoption in the Catholic digest and decided to inquire about this little boy for adoption through the Archdiocese adoption center. After many months of legal filings, they were able to finalize for this young boy from across the ocean to be united with his new forever family. His journey of being flown from Malta to New York City and then through the rigors of immigration, he was to finally be united with his new family in Pueblo Colorado. While on his voyage to the United States an interpreter was made available to assist Charles in getting acquainted with his new parents, sister and brother. For the next two years Charles courageously endured many challenges from learning the culture, and the language, the customs of the American people. It was daunting at best, but with the help of many families and friends, Charles started to adjust beautifully.

Charles had two siblings, one brother, Bill who was four months older than him and a sister, Kathy who was two years younger. Charles went to a Catholic parochial school until sixth grade and unknowingly it was discovered that he had a learning disability. His adopted family was able to send him to a private school in Evergreen, Colorado that could meet his needs. This private school had at that time, 22 boys who had similar learning challenges, including language, math, spelling etc. After about two years later Charles went to a public school in Evergreen where he embraced other students in his own age group and was now able to grasp everything the school had to offer in the learning curriculum. After Charles graduated from 9th grade he went back to Pueblo and to attend Pueblo Centennial High school and successfully graduated with a "B" average. In January of 1962, Charles became an American citizen which was reported in the *Pueblo Chieftain*. This was a very proud day for him.

The day Charles graduated from high school, he enlisted into the U. S. Navy. Charles did his boot camp training in San Diego, California. After boot camp, he was sent to culinary commissary cooking school to receive further training. After about 13 weeks he graduated and shipped out for active duty as a commissary man aboard a repair ship *The USS Amphion* in Norfolk, Virginia. He successfully and whole heartedly prepared meals for about 800 Navy men for approximately a year and then was transferred to the Officers' Quarters to cook for approximately 30 Officers and an Admiral. After two years of service, he was given an honorable discharge with a four-year active duty.

Soon after the military Charles decided he wanted to go into the restaurant business, so he began working in Denver, Colorado for numerous small restaurants and hotels as a busboy, waiter, and cook or anything they needed, Charles was happy to learn. He passionately worked in many fine dining establishments such as the Albany Hotel, Writers' Manor, Top of the Rockies, The Quorum Restaurant, The Brown Palace, The Broadmoor Hotel and The Trinity Grille just to name a few. While working at The Trinity Grille across from The Brown Palace, he found out about a new culinary school that would be the first to open in Denver area. He knew he not only had a passion, but a true gift for cooking, so he excitedly enrolled at The Art Institute of Colorado Culinary School. This new adventure was a two-year program with an Associate Degree designation.

During the time he was attending the school he had to learn the skills of becoming a chef. The program consisted of basic knowledge of kitchen equipment, knife skills, sauces, soups, and other basic recipes. During the next 5 quarters, baking, Garde Manager, wine & spirits, cost control, designing a restaurant, art, food language and ethnic food culture were covered. The classes started at 8:00 am until 3:00 pm, five days a week, all the while Charles was working part time for Dougal's catering service, plus studying for 2 hours a day. This was all a challenge for him, but he got through it all. The day of graduation they proudly announced Charles as the top of "The President's List" for Outstanding Achievement in all around academic field of the culinary business! He was so very surprised and appreciative to receive this award and so was his family who attended his graduation.

When he started the culinary program there were 150 students enlisted and by the end of the second quarter the enrollment dropped by a considerable amount. On the day of the graduation, there were 47 that graduated. Charles believed that a lot of the students, when they started the culinary program thought it was going to be easy, but it wasn't. There was so much to learn in a very little time but through it all he made it. Additionally, during his training in the culinary program he got a chance to meet a famous Chef from France, Chef Paul Bocuse who came to the school to give the thumbs up to the way the school was running the program. Chef Paul then shook Charles's hand and told him that he would be a great chef because of his smile and enthusiasm. Chef Bocuse then proceeded to sign Charles' professional chef cookbook.

Pour Charles
avec mes compliments
Paul Bocuse
1994

Foreword

During my visit to The Culinary Institute of America in Hyde Park, New York in 1989, I had the opportunity to see and appreciate the training methods applied at the school, which make it one of the best in the world.

A structured education yields excellent results, leading the students to the honorable title of "Professional Chef."

I remain convinced that respect for tradition in the teaching of culinary arts will be made most effective by enabling students to perfectly master the fundamental techniques. This approach to teaching, as featured in *The New Professional Chef*, finally provides the marketplace with chefs who know how to roast, grill, prepare proper mise en place, and are ready to address all of the specific needs of their profession.

Once more, all my congratulations to the Institute.

Paul Bocuse

Paul Bocuse

After Charles graduated from the culinary school, he then took his portfolio and applied to many places which were impressed but had no current openings. One day as he was walking up 17th Avenue in Denver, he came across an old stately building, and it said "The University Club" which was built in 1891. It was at that point he decided to check out this historical building where he noted a great aroma coming from it, in fact it was heavenly. Charles then walked in the back of the restaurant and found the kitchen. He then asked to speak to the Executive Chef, who took time to sit with Charles to hold a personal interview. The Executive Chef was impressed but sadly said that there was no full-time position, but he did have a part time position working in the pantry. Charles accepted whole heartedly not knowing that in three short weeks later he was hired for a full-time position as a Garde Manager Chef. Charles was now tasked to prepare cold food such as appetizers, soup, salads, sauces, and desserts. He also frequently worked behind the line cooking entrees, soups, sauces and sometimes breakfast.

He successfully worked many events at the club, but one of the biggest events was held during "The National Western Stock Show" that happened each January that was a theatrical program called "The 12th Night". It was a take off of a spoof of something; typically, it lasted for about a month. The first couple of weeks during this event the members of the club would rehearse each night. The night of the show, the members performed for the audience and after the show there was a parade of food ushered by the chefs through the entire theatre and then to the banquet room where the audience feasted on a whole roast pig, lobster, crab, shrimp galore, plus there was plenty of spirits to be had until the last man standing which was about 1:00 am in the morning.

During the 15 years that Charles was in their employ, he took a leave of absence to help a friend and became an Executive Chef in Saratoga, Wyoming. His friend had called upon Charles to replace the previous Executive Chef who mysteriously abandoned the restaurant leaving them in dire straits. By the end of the summer, now almost 6 months, Charles brought the business back to life as he was able to use his culinary training to monitor food cost which was not being managed by the previous chef. Charles enjoyed his time at the restaurant, but he quickly found out that small town living was not for him and he returned to The University Club and took over where he left off and they were so happy to have him back!

Charles truly enjoyed his career as a chef, but in addition to his interest in cooking, he was able to meet interesting people that he worked for on special occasions, like one well known American billionaire businessman in Denver, Mr. Phil Anschutz. At one time he worked for Mr. Anschutz on the weekends on his private railroad cars which were hooked up to the Rio Grande Railroad. The job consisted of taking care of his entourage in his private box cars as a waiter and cook while going from the Denver Union Train Station up to Winter Park and back in one full day. They loaded up the provisions for the day in the box car kitchen at 5:00 am in the morning and they were ready to greet the guests as they came aboard at 6:00 am. A continental breakfast was served as the train started its majestic journey to Winter Park Ski Resort. As the train approached the town of Winter Park the guests would exit to spend a full day of skiing or relaxing in the village.

With the departure of the guests for the day, the train headed off to Fraser, Colorado to dock for the day and the team began to prepare the evening meal. In the late afternoon, the train returned to Winter Park to pick up the guests. When the guests arrived, they were greeted in the private car with cocktails and appetizers in the beautiful viewing dome car and then later ushered to the private dining car for a fine dining experience with white tablecloths and vintage wine. Once the guests had finished their dinner the team had time to "wash the dishes" and put everything back in place in the kitchen car. At about 7:00 in the evening, we were now approaching Union Station back in downtown Denver. You could say it was a long 14-hour day but so fun and entertaining. Mr. Phil Anschutz and guests had a lovely day, and he was so kind to all of the staff.

During Charles's interest in the hotel restaurant business, he met many celebrities and other wonderful guests that he waited on at The Brown Palace such as Jimmy Stewart, Robert Six and his wife Audrey Meadows, Jane and Henry Fonda (and family), Carol Channing, the Shah of Iran and many others. In 1988, he also had the privilege to open and work at the five-star resort The Phoenician Resort in Scottsdale Arizona, on Camel Back Mountain owned by the infamous Charles Keating. He enjoyed working there until the government seized the resort in 1990 when Charles Keating was then sent to jail for one of the largest Savings and Loan scandals in the United States.

In 2011 Charles retired from The University Club and he decided to become a dedicated volunteer for a non-profit called 'Project Angel Heart'. He worked tirelessly in the kitchen preparing and serving meals for over 1,300 people with varying medical issues. After a couple years working in the kitchen Charles decided to, in his own words, "Give my poor old feet a break . . ." and he transferred his volunteer work from the kitchen to the front desk answering phone calls, directing people and various other positions wherever they needed him. Charles was an invaluable volunteer, loved by everyone and touched the lives of thousands of people in need. During the time that he was volunteering at Angel Heart he created a large mural shaped into a heart out of old Angel Heart buttons. The buttons represented the mission of Angel Heart, providing clients with food to nourish their health, mind, and physical being. This beautiful piece of art still hangs proudly in their board room.

In addition to working at Project Angel Heart, Charles spent thousands of hours doing fundraisers for charity organizations, doing fundraiser Six Course Dinners for different organizations such as Angel Heart, Father Woody's Haven of Hope, Machebeuf High School, Blessed Sacrament Church, and others where he raised $500.00 to $2,000 for the formal dinners he put on at his home for up to a dozen people Every guest got the Royal Five Star service starting with cocktails, appetizers, and a full six course dinner. One of the specialties Charles enjoyed offering was that each guest had a typed out "fancy menu" to take home to show their friends what a wonderful meal and experience they had.

Over the years, Charles has helped raise over $50,000 and that is a low estimate! To this day he still enjoys cooking for other people, especially for his friends. Charles tries to stay current with different cooking techniques and recipes. He also enjoys the cooking channels, watching the chefs prepare food, using new culinary skills and techniques, as well as the experienced chefs from the past. For him, being a chef is in his blood and to see a happy guest leaving his table with a satisfied look on their faces knowing that they truly enjoyed the meal is a happy accomplishment for him. Additionally, when they leave the table, they will talk about this meal and or event for years to come, as an amazing culinary experience.

Charles would like to close his journey in the hospitality business by saying to you, "whether you are a waiter, cook, or chef, it will always be rewarded back to you tenfold," so take this journey as did he and see where it will take you.

Bon Appetit . . .

Chef Charles McDonald

10 Steps for a Successful Dinner Party

1. Plan a date and select a menu for your special occasion dinner party.
2. Send invitations by mail, electronically or by telephone.
3. Go over the menu at least one week in advance to determine what ingredients you will need. First check your pantry, your refrigerator and freezer for what you have on hand and then create a list of what to purchase at the grocery store and/or meat market or online shopping.
4. Create a shopping list and organize into categories:
   - Seafood
   - Dairy
   - Meat
   - Poultry
   - Produce
   - Bakery
   - Deli
   - Dry goods
   - Canned goods
   - Spices
   - Floral
   - Miscellaneous

5. Locate all your serving plates, serving dishes, utensils and make sure they are clean and ready.
6. The day before the party/event begin prepping anything that can be done ahead, for example: chopping vegetables, making appetizers, soups, entrée, starches and desserts.
7. The day before: set your table starting with a festive tablecloth, silverware, napkins, plates, bowls, water glasses, wine glasses, floral arrangements, decorations, name tents, menus, etc.
8. The morning of the party make a list of everything that needs to be done from start to finish prior to the guests arriving – don't forget about "to go" boxes for leftover take aways too!
9. Keep your kitchen organized by washing pans and dishes throughout the day – putting everything back into place will keep your counters clear and your cooking stress free!
10. Just before the guests arrive, fill the water glasses with ice and water.

Enjoy and Bon Appetit

Menus with Recipes for International & Occasional Cuisines

New Year's Day

1st Course
Shrimp Edamame with Sauce Americana

2nd Course
Avocado and Crab Soup

3rd Course
Watercress, Radish and Onion Salad with
Poppyseed Vinaigrette

4th Course
Chicken Bismark with Jasmine Rice

5th Course
Almond Bourbon Honey Cake

Suggested Wine
Kendall Jackson Chardonnay

Valentine's Day

1st Course

Beggars Purse Filled Shrimp with Romesco Sauce

2nd Course

Hearts of Palm Salad with Maltese Sauce

3rd Course

Pistachio Crusted Pork Tenderloin with Jalapeno Plum Sauce
Serve with Fresh Asparagus & Chive Mashed Potatoes

4th Course

Snickerdoodle Cheesecake with Chocolate Sauce

Suggested Wine

Beringer White Zinfandel

St. Patrick's Day

1st Course
Oven Baked Scotch Egg

2nd Course
Cream of Celeriac Soup

3rd Course
Arugula Watercress Salad with Lemon Vinaigrette Dressing

4th Course
Corned Beef and Cabbage with Fall Vegetables

5th Course
Key Lime Pie with Mango Cream Sauce

Suggested Wine
Beaujolais Village

Easter Day

1st Course
Rainbow Trout with Jalapeno Corn Sauce

2nd Course
Roasted Acorn Squash and Pear Soup

3rd Course
Celeriac & Radish Salad with Louis Dressing

4th Course
Peach Mint Coconut Granita

5th Course
Chicken Stuffed with Herb Pimento Cream Cheese
With Roasted Red Potatoes and Broccolini

6th Course
Coconut Almond Cream Cake

Suggested Wine
Pinot Grigio

Springtime

1st Course

Senegalese Soup

2nd Course

Jicama Walnut Apple & Fig Salad with Thai Dressing

3rd Course

Salmon Wrapped Puff Pastry with Saffron Sauce
Served with Medley of Fresh Steamed Herb Vegetables

4th Course

Lemon Blueberry Cake with Lemon Curd

Suggested Wine

Blu Vin White Riesling

Cinco de Mayo

1st Course
Shrimp Empanadas with Pineapple Jalapeno Salsa

2nd Course
Creamy Black Bean Soup

3rd Course
Prickly Pear Granita

4th Course
Shredded Duck Chili Rellenos

5th Course
Mexican Chocolate Tart with Almond Cream Anglaise

Suggested Wine
Zinfandel

Juneteenth

1st Course
New Orleans Crab Cakes with Siracha Cream Corn Sauce

2nd Course
Cream of Fennel Soup

3rd Course
Cornmeal Crusted Catfish with Jalapeno Cilantro Sauce
With Sautéed Collar Greens, Fried Okra & Cornbread

4th Course
Banana Foster Pecan Cream Brulée

Suggested Beverage
Southern Strawberry Iced Tea

Summer in the City

1st Course
Lamb Satay with Peanut Sauce

2nd Course
Waterzooi Soup

3rd Course
Arizona Cactus Salad with Honey Lime Vinaigrette

4th Course
Chicken Scaloppini with Artichoke Caper Lemon Sauce
Serve with Steamed White Rice and Orange Glazed Carrots

5th Course
Apple Spice Cake with Cranberry Sauce

Suggested Wine
William Hill Chardonnay

Fourth of July

1st Course
Sweet Potato & Chorizo Empanada with Cilantro Sauce

2nd Course
Mango, Avocado & Goat Cheese Salad with Mango Vinaigrette

3rd Course
Salmon Wrapped Phyllo with Mornay Sauce
Served with Garlic Herb Orzo & Parmesan Buttered Broccoli

4th Course
Sour Orange Pie

Suggested Wine
Sauvignon Blanc

Hot Month of August

1st Course
Indian Curry Shrimp and Scallop Crepes

2nd Course
Coconut Curry Lentil Soup

3rd Course
Pomegranate & Persimmon Salad

4th Course
Jamaican Chicken with Papaya & Mango Salsa

5th Course
Cranberry Almond Pudding with Almond Butter Sauce

Suggested Wine
Chenin Blanc

Start of Fall

1st Course

Chic Pea Fritter Cakes with Tahina Dip

2nd Course

Apple Butternut Squash Bisque with Roasted Chestnuts

3rd Course

Poached Pear Stuffed Gorgonzola & Champagne Dressing

4th Course

Italian Short Ribs with Parmesan Polenta

5th Course

Pumpkin Oreo Pie Parfait

Suggested Wine

Gewurztraminer Wine

Special Occasion

1st Course
Artichoke and Shrimp Cream Brulée

2nd Course
Senegalese Soup

3rd Course
Lentil and Cucumber Salad with Crumble Feta Cheese

4th Course
Blueberry Lemon Granita

5th Course
Mandarin Orange Dijon Chicken

6th Course
Chocolate Pecan Pumpkin Rum Cake

Suggested Wine
Sauvignon Blanc

Thanksgiving Day

1st Course
Baked Rollatini of Sole with Puttanesca Sauce

2nd Course
Pumpkin Apple Bisque Soup

3rd Course
Farro and Roasted Eggplant Salad

4th Course
Stuffed Turkey Roulade with Sage Mushroom Sauce

5th Course
No Bake Pumpkin Pecan Cheesecake

Suggested Wine
Pinot Grigio

Christmas Dinner

1st Course

Salmon Cake with Raspberry Chipotle Sauce

2nd Course

Pumpkin and Sage Soup

3rd Course

Hearts of Palm Salad with Maltese Sauce

4th Course

Peach Sangria Granita

5th Course

Stuffed Peppercorn Crusted Pork Tenderloin

6th Course

Cranberry Almond Pudding with Almond Butter Sauce

Suggested Wine

Beringer Chardonnay

American Dining

1st Course
Shrimp Edamame with Sauce Americana

2nd Course
Old English Scallop Chowder

3rd Course
*Mango, Avocado and Goat Cheese Salad
with Mango Vinaigrette*

4th Course
English Braised Short Ribs with Polenta or Butter Noodles

5th Course
Oreo Mint Chocolate Jelly Roll with Cream de Menthe Sauce

Suggested Wine
Beringer Chardonnay

Anniversary

1st *Course*

Southwestern Lobster Cake with Aioli Sauce

2nd **Course**

Peruvian Potato Soup

3rd **Course**

Pomegranate and Persimmon Salad

4th **Course**

Pork Tenderloin – Grilled with Mediterranean Salsa

5th **Course**

Mocha Cheesecake with Pecans

Suggested Wine

Veuve Clicquot Champagne

Happy Birthday

1st Course

Asian Shrimp Cocktail

2nd Course

Cream of Chicken Alfredo Soup

3rd Course

Hawaiian Tropical Carrot & Coconut Salad

4th Course

Chicken Stuffed with Capicola Blue Cheese with Mushroom Sauce. Served with Chive Orzo Rice and Glazed Honey Carrots.

5th Course

Fudge Truffle Cheesecake

Suggested Wine

Pinot Grigio

Asian Dining

1st Course
Thai Shrimp Cakes with Jalapeno Plum Sauce

2nd Course
Ginger Carrot Soup

3rd Course
Kimchi Noodle Salad on Rice Cake Bowl

4th Course
Sweet Chili Lychee Ginger Granita

5th Course
Thai Salmon with Bangkok Curry Sauce
Serve with Steamed Rice & Sautéed Snow Peas

6th Course
Chinese Five Spice Cake with Ginger Cream Sauce

Suggested Wine
Sauvignon Blanc

Formal & Fine Dining

1st Course
Oven Baked Scotch Egg

2nd Course
Wild Mushroom Soup

3rd Course
Honeydew Mint Granita

4th Course
Cornmeal Crusted Tilapia with Puttanesca Sauce

5th Course
Meyer Lemon and Thyme Cream Brulée

Suggested Wine
Gewurztraminer

French Dining

1ˢᵗ Course
Sweet Onion Tartlet

*2ⁿᵈ **Course***
Creamy Louisiana Crawfish Bisque

*3ʳᵈ **Course***
Pink Grapefruit Granita

*4ᵗʰ **Course***
Salmon en Papillot with Lemon Herb Couscous and
Fresh Grilled Asparagus with Creamy Mustard Sauce

*5ᵗʰ **Course***
Coconut Almond Cream Cake

Suggested Wine
Sauvignon Blanc

Gay Pride

1ˢᵗ Course
English Sausage Roll

2ⁿᵈ Course
Roasted Garlic and Spinach Soup

3ʳᵈ Course
Asian Carrot Slaw in Waffle Bowl

4ᵗʰ Course
Chicken Stuffed Artichoke with Bechamel Sauce

5ᵗʰ Course
Snickerdoodle Cheesecake with Chocolate Sauce

Suggested Wine
Beringer White Zinfandel

Italian Dining

1st Course
Shrimp Manicotti with Pesto Sauce

2nd Course
Roasted Garlic and Spinach Soup

3rd Course
Farro and Roasted Eggplant Salad

4th Course
Watermelon Granita

5th Course
Osso Buco with Gremolata

6th Course
Italian Cream Cake

Suggested Wine
Pinot Grigio

Tex Mex

1st Course
Stuffed Shrimp Poblano with Tomatillo Sauce

2nd Course
Cream of Avocado & Black Bean Soup

3rd Course
Peach Sangria Granita

4th Course
Chorizo Stuffed with Black Bean Sauce

5th Course
Mexican Chocolate Tart with Almond Cream Anglaise

Suggested Wine
Dry Riesling

New England

1st Course
Southwestern Lobster Cake with Aioli Sauce

2nd Course
Boston Fish Chowder

3rd Course
Red & Yellow Roasted Beet Salad with Pistachio & Goat Cheese

4th Course
Lobster Thermidor and Boston Brown Bread

5th Course
Black Bottom Pie

Suggested Wine
Sauvignon Blanc

Appetizers . . .

- ❖ *Artichoke and Shrimp Creme Brulée*
- ❖ *Asian Chicken Meatballs with Sweet Asian Sauce*
- ❖ *Asian Shrimp Cocktail*
- ❖ *Baked Rollatini of Sole with Puttanesca Sauce*
- ❖ *Beggars Purse Filled with Shrimp & Romesco Sauce*
- ❖ *Chic Pea Fritter Cakes with Tahina Dip*
- ❖ *Crab and Shrimp Shooter*
- ❖ *English Sausage Roll*
- ❖ *Indian Curry Shrimp and Scallop Crepes*
- ❖ *Lamb Satay with Peanut Sauce*
- ❖ *New Orleans Crab Cakes with Siracha Cream Corn Sauce*
- ❖ *Oven Baked Scotch Egg*
- ❖ *Rainbow Trout with Jalapeno Corn Sauce*
- ❖ *Salmon Cakes with Raspberry Chipotle Sauce*
- ❖ *Shredded Duck Chili Rellenos*
- ❖ *Shrimp Edamame with Sauce Americana*
- ❖ *Shrimp Empanadas with Pineapple Jalapeno Salsa*
- ❖ *Shrimp Manicotti with Marinara and Pesto Sauce*
- ❖ *Southwestern Lobster Cake with Aioli Sauce*
- ❖ *Stuffed Shrimp Poblano with Tomatillo Sauce*
- ❖ *Sweet Onion Tartlet*
- ❖ *Sweet Potato and Chorizo Empanada with Cilantro Sauce*
- ❖ *Thai Shrimp Cakes with Jalapeno Sauce*

Artichoke and Shrimp Crème Brulée

Ingredients

- 1 can 8-ounce artichoke drained and chopped
- 1 cup cooked, and shelled shrimp chopped
- 1 garlic clove minced
- 1/4 cup finely diced yellow onion
- 2 cups cream
- 3 large eggs
- ¼ teaspoon nutmeg
- Salt and pepper to taste
- ¼ cup grated parmesan cheese

Putting It All Together

- Preheat oven to 350 degrees
- Sauté onions and garlic with 2 tablespoon olive oil in a skillet
- Mix artichoke and shrimp together with onions and garlic
- In another bowl add eggs and cream and whisk then add the
- Remaining ingredients, except the cheese
- Butter 4 ramekins and add the mixture into the ramekins
- Carefully pour water in a large baking pan ½ up to the ramekins
- Bake 45 minutes or until it sets in center, cool ramekins and top
- With cheese, torch with flame till lightly brown and serve warm

Serves 4 people

Asian Chicken Meatballs

Ingredients - Meatball

- 1-pound ground chicken
- 1 cup panko breadcrumbs
- 2 eggs
- 1 tablespoon fresh grated ginger
- 3 tablespoons soy sauce
- 3 tablespoons finely chopped green scallion
- 3 tablespoons finely chopped parsley
- Sprinkle of sesame seeds for garnish
- Chopped parsley for garnish

Ingredients - Sauce

- 3/4 cup hoisin sauce
- ¼ cup brown sugar
- 4 tablespoons soy sauce
- 4 tablespoons rice wine vinegar
- 2 tablespoons sweet Asian sauce
- 1 tablespoon grated ginger

Putting the Asian Sauce Together

- Stir together all the ingredients in a small saucepan until it comes to a boil
- Turn the heat down and simmer for 5 minutes
- Pour sauce over meatballs and sprinkle sesame seeds on top and
- Put on to a 5-inch wooden skewers

Putting It All Together

- Preheat oven to 350 degrees
- Mix all the meatball ingredients into a bowl and stir until fully mixed
- Use a small cookie scoop and make the mini meatballs
- Put onto a sheet pan and bake for approximately 15 minutes
- Take meatballs out of the oven and pour the Asian sauce over meatballs
- Garnish with a sprinkle of sesame seeds and chopped parsley

Serves 4 people

Asian Shrimp Cocktail

Ingredients

- 12-ounce uncooked medium shrimp with tail on
- Toss shrimp with 1 tablespoon of olive oil and 1 teaspoon of
- Sesame oil

Putting Shrimp Together

- Heat skillet add the mix oil and shrimp cook until pink and remove
- From heat and cool

Ingredients - Asian cocktail sauce

- 1 small clove finely minced garlic
- 1 tablespoon rice wine vinegar
- 1 cup of mayonnaise
- 1 teaspoon sesame oil
- 1 tablespoon soy sauce
- ¼ cup sweet chili sauce
- 1 teaspoon lea and per
- 1 tablespoon each lemon and lime juice
- 1 tablespoon finely chopped cilantro
- 1 teaspoon fresh grated ginger
- Salt and pepper to taste
- 4 sprigs of fresh cilantro leaves for garnish

Putting the Sauce Together

Mix all the ingredients of Asian cocktail sauce together and serve individual champagne glasses and place the shrimp on top of the sauce and garnish with cilantro leaves.

Serves 4 people

Baked Rollatini of Sole with Puttanesca Sauce

Ingredients

- 6 fillets of sole about 1 ½ pounds skinless
- ¼ cup finely chopped parsley
- 2 tablespoons dry oregano
- ¼ cup dry breadcrumbs
- 3 tablespoons melted butter
- ¼ cup Parmigiana Cheese
- 1 cup dry white wine
- Chopped parsley for garnish

Prepare to Cook

- Sprinkle parsley and oregano over the 6 sole
- Roll each sole into a cylinder and brush the tops with butter, breadcrumbs and cheese
- Lay the sole into a shallow dish, pour the dry white wine in the dish and bake for 20 minutes
- Serve with Puttanesca sauce and garnish with chopped parsley

Ingredients - Puttanesca Sauce

- ¼ cup olive oil 2 tablespoon tomato paste
- 1 cup chopped onion 2 tablespoon drained capers
- 2 (28 ounce) can of plum tomatoes 2 tablespoons minced anchovy fillet
- 1 cup of pitted Kalamata olives chopped ½ teaspoon each basil and red pepper flakes
- 6 cloves garlic minced Salt and Pepper to taste

Putting It All Together

- In a large pot add olive oil over medium heat
- Add onions and garlic and sauté about 5 minutes
- Cook for 2 minutes, add tomatoes and the rest of the ingredients
- Simmer till sauce has thickened, about 30 minutes
- Adjust seasoning to taste

Serves 4-6 people

Beggars Purses Filled with Shrimp & Romesco Sauce

Ingredients

- 1 ½ cups cooked shrimp diced fine
- ½ teaspoon old bay seasoning
- 1 tablespoon fresh chop chives
- 4 scallions blanched and reserve to tie the purses
- Salt and pepper to taste
- Sprig of parsley for garnish

Ingredients - Crepe for beggars purses

- 1/2 cup all-purpose flour
- ½ cup whole milk
- ¼ cup water
- 2 eggs
- 2 tablespoons unsalted butter melted
- Pinch of salt

Ingredients - Romesco Sauce

- 1 ½ ounces of roasted pepper
- 4 small plum tomatoes
- 1 cup raw almonds
- ¼ cup fresh parsley
- ¼ cup olive oil
- 2 cloves of garlic
- Juice of ½ lemon
- Salt and pepper to taste

Putting Sauce together

- Take all the ingredients and put into a blender, pulse until smooth
- When ready to serve warm the Romesco sauce
- Serve with the beggars purse or any chicken, fish, or vegetables

Putting It All Together

- Mix the crepe ingredients together and chill for 30 minutes
- Heat an 8-inch nonstick sauté pan and brush a little with melted butter
- Take ¼ cup batter into the pan and swirl to coat the entire pan evenly
- Cook the crepe till the bottom is set and golden brown
- Flip the crepe over and finish till it is lightly brown
- Continue till you should have 12 crepes
- Take each crepe and put 1 dollop (approximately 2 Tablespoons) of shrimp filling in the middle of each crepe
- Draw together the sides to resemble a purse and tie each one with a scallion strip
- When ready to serve heat in oven at 350F for 15 minutes
- Put a dollop of Romesco sauce on plate; add beggars purse and sprig of parsley for garnish

Serves 4-6 people

Chickpea Fritter Cakes with Tzatziki Dip

Ingredients

- 1 can (15 ½ ounce) Garbanzo Beans rinsed and drained
- 4 tablespoons Tahini paste
- ¼ cup chopped onions
- ¼ cup can diced tomato
- 1 garlic clove minced
- 1 teaspoon cumin
- ¼ teaspoon each Salt and Pepper
- 1 teaspoon paprika
- 1 teaspoon cumin
- ¼ teaspoon cayenne
- 6 Mint leaves chopped
- Flour to dredge cakes
- Olive Oil
- Chopped parsley for garnish
- Serve with warm Pita bread

Putting It All Together

- In a blender ruff chop all the ingredients except flour and oil
- When combined add little flour if needed to shape into individual 2-inch cakes
- Roll and shape the cakes; dredge each one lightly with flour
- Heat a sauté pan with vegetable oil; when hot lay the cakes gently
- Fry each side till golden brown; remove the cakes from oil and lay on paper towel
- Serve with Tzatziki Sauce and garnish with chopped parsley

Ingredients - Tzatziki Dip

- ¾ English cucumber partially peeled, and seeds removed from the center and diced into small cubes
- 1 teaspoon Kosher Salt
- 4 to 5 Garlic cloves peeled and finely minced
- 1 teaspoon white vinegar
- 2 cups of plain Greek Yogurt
- ¼ teaspoon white pepper

Putting It All Together

- Mix all the ingredients and serve with warm Pita bread

Makes 20 Chickpea Fritter Cakes

Crab and Shrimp Shooter

Ingredients

- 6 large shrimp cooked and chopped into small pieces
- 1 lb. of lump crab (check for bones)
- 2 Roma tomatoes diced
- 1 stalk of celery finely diced
- Small head of shredded lettuce
- Sprigs of fresh parsley for garnish
- Lemon wedges for garnish

Ingredients - Avocado Sauce

- 1 ripe avocado cut into small pieces
- 2 tablespoons mayonnaise
- 2 tablespoons chopped scallion cut into small pieces
- ½ finely chopped celery
- 1 Tsp Cajun seasoning
- Mix all the ingredients and set aside

Ingredients - Creole Sauce

- 1 cup of mayonnaise
- 1 tablespoon finely chopped shallot
- 2 tablespoons finely chopped parsley
- ½ finely chopped celery
- ¼ teaspoon Cajun seasoning
- 1 tablespoon creole mustard or Dijon mustard
- 1 teaspoon smoked paprika
- ½ teaspoon lea and Perrins
- 1 teaspoon fresh lemon juice
- Mix all the ingredients and set aside

Putting It All Together

- To assemble start with a slender parfait glass
- Layer small amount of shredded lettuce
- Add creole sauce
- Add small amount of crab top with small amount of diced tomato
- Add lettuce top with avocado sauce on top with diced shrimp and diced tomato
- Repeat when finished and top with garnish of sprig of fresh parsley

Serves 4-6 people

English Sausage Roll

Ingredients

- 2 sheets frozen puff pastry
- 2 eggs slightly beaten
- 1 ½ lbs. sausage
- 1 onion diced fine
- 2 cloves garlic finely diced
- 2 tablespoons chop parsley
- 2 tablespoons chop fresh thyme
- 1 cup panko breadcrumbs
- Salt and pepper to taste

Putting It All Together

- Preheat oven to 350
- Cut the 2-puff pastry long length
- Brush the edges w/ little of the beaten egg
- Mix remaining eggs with the remaining ingredients in a large bowl
- Divide the mixture with the 4 halves of the puff pastry
- Brush the edges of the puff pastry and fold the pastry over the filling
- With a fork crimp down all the way around the pastry
- Brush the entire puff pastry with an egg wash
- Place the puff pastry roll on a greased baking sheet
- Place in oven and bake for ½ hour or until golden brown
- When done take out of oven and let it rest
- Slice puff pastry in small bite size pieces
- Any left-over sausage roll can be wrapped tightly and put in the freezer

Serve the English Sausage Rolls with your favorite sauce:

- Marinara Sauce
- Bechamel Sauce
- Mustard Sauce
- Pesto Sauce
- Vodka Sauce

Any of these sauces above are great for the holidays or any other times.

Serves 6-8 people

Indian Curry Shrimp and Scallop Crepes

Ingredients

- ½ pound bay scallops
- ½ pound medium cooked shrimp peeled and tail off
- 1 thin cut carrot length wise julienne style
- 1 thin cut celery rib length wise julienne style
- Small amount snow peas cut length wise julienne style
- 2 tablespoons flour
- 3 tablespoons unsalted butter
- 1 cup milk
- ¼ teaspoon nutmeg
- 2 teaspoons curry powder
- ½ squeezed lemon
- Salt and pepper to taste
- Shredded mint leaves for garnish

Prepare to cook

- Steam carrots, celery, and snow peas till tender
- In a small pot melt butter and add flour to make a roux cook for 3 minutes
- Add milk and curry and whisk in a stream till smooth
- Add salt and pepper to taste and squeeze ½ lemon
- Stir in the seafood and vegetables to the curry sauce and set aside to fill crepes

Ingredients - Bechamel Sauce

- 2 tablespoons butter
- 2 tablespoons flour
- 1 ¼ cup milk heated
- ¼ teaspoon salt
- ¼ teaspoon nutmeg

Putting It All Together

- Melt butter in a saucepan
- Add flour and cook, stirring constantly until it has thickened, about 2 minutes
- Add hot milk continuing to stir as sauce thickens, reduce heat

Add salt and nutmeg to taste – remove from heat and keep warm till serves time

Ingredients - Crepe Batter

- 1 ½ cups milk
- 2 large eggs lightly beaten
- 1 cup all-purpose flour
- 1 tablespoon sugar
- ¼ teaspoon salt
- Cooking spray

Prepare the batter

- Mix the milk and eggs together in a bowl and then add the flour, sugar and salt
- Make the crepe in a six-inch saucepan sprayed with cooking spray until crepe starts to bubble, flip and cook the other side until lightly brown on the bottom, less than one minute and repeat for the remaining batter

Putting It All Together

- Put the filling in each crepe and roll and place in a 9X9 glass dish sprayed with cooking spray
- Top with a bechamel sauce
- Cook for 30 minutes at 350 degrees

Garnish with shredded min leaves and serve.

Serves 4-6 people

Lamb Satay with Peanut Sauce

Ingredients

- 4 loin lamb chops
- Trim the lamb of any excess fat and cut the loin cross wise into 1-inch cubes
- 4-6 skewers 6 inch each
- Chopped parsley for garnish

Ingredients - Peanut Sauce for the Marinade

- 1 teaspoon lemon juice
- 2 tablespoons vegetable oil
- 2 cloves of garlic
- ¼ yellow onion chopped
- 1 star anise
- 2/3 cup creamy peanut butter
- ¼ cup vegetable oil
- ¼ cup soy sauce
- 1 tablespoon chopped fresh ginger
- 2 teaspoons ground cumin
- 2 tablespoons fresh lime juice
- 2 teaspoons chili sauce
- 2 tablespoons soy sauce
- ¾ cup coconut milk
- 1 teaspoon chili powder
- 1 teaspoon sugar

Mix all the above ingredients in a bowl and set aside and place lamb to marinade for 30 minutes to an hour in the refrigerator.

Putting It All Together

- Remove the lamb from the bowl and reserve the marinade, thread the lamb onto skewers and place on a serving dish
- Process the marinade in the blender until smooth and cook in a sauté pan for 10 minutes and set aside
- Grill the lamb gently on medium heat for about 3 to 4 minutes on all sides
- Top the lamb with the peanut sauce and chopped parsley (or serve on the side)

Serves 4-6people

New Orleans Crab Cakes with Siracha Cream Corn Sauce

Ingredients

- ½ cup mayonnaise
- 1 large egg beaten
- 1 tablespoon creole mustard
- 1 tablespoon Lea and Perrin
- ½ teaspoon Cajun hot sauce
- 1 tablespoon creole seasoning
- 1-pound lump crab meat remove small bones
- 1 cup fine breadcrumbs
- ¼ cup canola oil for frying
- Chopped parsley for garnish

Ingredients - Siracha Cream Corn Sauce

- 1 cup (16 ounce) can of cream corn
- 1 tablespoon butter
- ½ cup chopped yellow onion
- ¼ cup each of red and green bell pepper finely chopped
- 1 tablespoon finely chopped jalapeno
- ½ teaspoon creole seasoning
- 1 tablespoon siracha
- ¼ cup sour cream

Putting the Sauce Together
- Sauté onions, bell peppers and jalapeno for a few minutes
- Add the rest of the ingredients and stir well

Putting It All Together

- In a bowl whisk the first 6 ingredients
- Fold the crab and breadcrumbs gently into the mayonnaise mixture
- Shape into 4 inch 'cake' patties; cover and refrigerate for 1 hour
- Heat oil in skillet; sauté the crab cakes on both sides till golden brown
- Top with Siracha Cream Corn Sauce and chopped parsley for garnish

Serves 4-6 people

Oven Baked Scotch Egg

Ingredients

- 1 lb. pork sausage
- 1 teaspoon minced onion
- 1 garlic clove minced
- 1 teaspoon of dry thyme
- Salt and pepper to taste
- All-purpose flour for dredging
- Panko breadcrumbs for breading
- 1 egg beaten
- 4 hardboiled eggs

Putting It All Together

- Heat oven to 350 degrees
- In a large bowl mix pork sausage, onion, garlic, thyme, salt and pepper
- Shape the mixture into 4 equal patties
- Roll the hard boil eggs in flour to coat
- Place on sausage patty and shape around egg
- Dip each egg into egg mixture and then breadcrumbs
- Cover completely
- Place on ungreased cookie sheet and bake 30 minutes
- Serve with creamy mustard sauce or by itself

Serves 4 people

Rainbow Trout with Jalapeno Sweet Corn Sauce

Ingredients

- 3 Rainbow Trout split all in half deboned by your fishmonger
- ¼ cup all-purpose flour
- ¼ teaspoon each salt and pepper
- 3 tablespoons butter
- 6 sprigs of cilantro

Putting It All Together

- Dust each ½ of the trout with flour
- Lightly salt and pepper trout
- Pan fry the trout skin down in a hot skillet in butter for 3-4 minutes, flip the trout over and do the same procedure
- Serve the trout with a wedge of lemon and a sauce of your choice or my Creamy Jalapeno Sweet Corn Sauce

Ingredients - Creamy Jalapeno Sweet Corn Sauce

- 1 can 15-ounce sweet corn
- 1 package 8-ounce cream cheese softened
- 2 Jalapenos seeded and finely diced
- ¼ cup butter
- Salt and pepper to taste

Put all the ingredients together in a medium pot cook slowly and stirring till well combined and then serve over the trout or on the side and top with a sprig of cilantro for each.

Serves 6 people with half-trout portions.

Salmon Cakes with Raspberry Chipotle Sauce

Ingredients

- 2 Pounds of fresh skinless and Boneless Salmon
- 1 onion finely diced
- 4 tablespoons panko breadcrumbs plus ½ cup for breading
- 1 large egg beaten
- 2 tablespoons mayonnaise
- 1 tablespoon finely chopped capers
- 2 tablespoons chopped chives
- 1 tablespoon Dijon mustard
- 1 ½ teaspoons fresh lemon juice
- 1 teaspoon hot sauce
- Salt and Pepper to taste
- Vegetable oil to fry cakes

Putting It All Together

- Chop salmon into small bite size pieces
- Sauté onion till lightly golden brown and set aside
- In a large bowl place salmon and remaining ingredients; mix until combined
- Shape the cakes into a disk with a 4-ounce scoop or ice cream scoop
- Dredge salmon cakes with the breadcrumbs and sauté in a medium hot skillet
- Cook cakes till golden brown on each side
- Place cakes onto a wire rack and serve warm

Ingredients - Raspberry Chipotle Sauce

- 1 tablespoon olive oil
- ½ cup diced onion
- 2 teaspoons minced garlic
- 2 teaspoons chipotle chilies in adobo
- 2 pints fresh raspberry
- ½ cup raspberry vinegar
- ¾ cup sugar
- ½ teaspoon salt

Putting It All Together

- Heat olive oil over medium heat in saucepan
- Add onions and cook until soft
- Add garlic and sauté for 1 minute
- Add chipotle and cook
- Add raspberry and cook 3 to 4 minutes
- Add vinegar and stir to deglaze pan
- Add sugar and salt
- Reduce the heat to medium until sauce has thickened – 8 to 10 minutes
- Strain sauce through a strainer press on solids to extract liquid
- Serve room temperature with a drizzle with raspberry chipotle sauce

Serves 4-6 people

Shredded Duck Chili Rellenos

Ingredients

- 2 duck breasts (8 ounce) cooked and shredded
- 4 medium size poblano peppers
- 1 teaspoon canola oil
- ½ medium onion diced fine
- 1 clove garlic finely minced
- 1 can 16-ounce diced tomatoes
- 1 jalapeno seeded and finely diced
- ¼ red bell pepper seeded and diced
- ¼ cup chopped fresh cilantro
- ½ teaspoon ground cumin
- ¼ cup softened cream cheese
- 1 teaspoon hot sauce
- 4 ounces pepper jack cheese
- Salt and pepper to taste
- Chopped parsley for garnish

Putting It All Together

- Preheat oven to 350 degrees
- Remove the skin off the duck breast
- Sear in a hot pan on both sides until internal temp of 165 degrees; let cool to rest
- Grill the poblano peppers under the broiler on all sides until blistered
- Take out of the broiler and split the peppers in half removing the seeds
- In a hot skillet sauté onions and garlic until soft
- Add the can of tomatoes, jalapeno, red bell pepper cilantro, shredded duck
- Add hot sauce to taste
- Once all the mixture is incorporated add the cheese
- Stuff the mixture in the poblano peppers and top with a pinch (1 oz each) of cheese
- Place the peppers in a shallow dish and bake in oven for 30 minutes,
- Remove once cooked all the way through and serve with a garnish of chopped parsley

Serves 4 people

Shrimp Edamame with Sauce Americana

Ingredients

- 24 ounces frozen ravioli
- 12 ounces medium cooked shrimp with tails off
- ½ cup frozen edamame cook as directed
- Chopped parsley for garnish

Ingredients - Americana Sauce

- 28 ounce can diced tomatoes
- 3 tablespoons of olive oil
- Teaspoon pepper flakes
- ¼ cup diced pancetta
- 3 cloves garlic finely minced
- 1 teaspoon red pepper flakes
- Salt and pepper to taste

Putting the Americana Sauce Together

- In a blender puree the tomatoes until smooth
- Heat olive oil in pan over medium heat and add pancetta until golden brown
- Add garlic and red pepper flakes
- Add the pureed tomatoes and basil, salt & pepper to taste
- Reduce heat to low stir well and cook for 15 minutes

Putting It All Together

- Boil the ravioli according to package; drain and set aside
- Sauté 12 ounces of cooked shrimp in light drizzle of olive oil and salt and pepper
- Boil the edamame 3 to 5 minutes; drain and set aside
- Mix the Americana sauce with the ravioli, shrimp and edamame and garnish with chopped parsley

Serves 4 people

Shrimp Empanadas with a Pineapple Jalapeno Salsa

Ingredients

- 1 box frozen pie dough
- 1 egg

Ingredients - Filling

- 10-ounce medium shrimp peeled with tail off
- 1 small onion finely diced
- 1 clove of garlic
- ½ each red and green bell pepper
- 4 ounce can green chili
- 1 small jalapeno finely diced
- 2 cups shredded pepper jack cheese
- ½ teaspoon each cumin and chili powder
- 1 tablespoon Mexican oregano
- Chopped cilantro for garnish

Ingredients - Pineapple Jalapeno Salsa

- 1 cup diced fresh pineapple 1 Tablespoon lime juice
- ½ small diced jalapeno 3 tablespoon fresh cilantro
- ½ cup chopped red onion Salt and Pepper to taste

Putting the Sauce Together

- Combine all the ingredients together in a bowl and mix
- Cover and chill until serving time

Putting It All Together

- Preheat oven to 350 degrees
- Thaw frozen pie dough and place on lightly floured surface
- Roll to 1/8-inch-thick; cut the dough in circles with a 3-inch cookie cutter
- Place a spoon full of shrimp filling in center of circles
- Fold the dough over the filling in half; crimp the edges with a fork
- Lay the empanadas on a sheet tray and brush each empanada with egg wash
- Bake for 20 to 25 minutes and serve hot with chopped cilantro for garnish

24 appetizer servings

Shrimp Manicotti with Marinara and Pesto Sauce

Ingredients

- 8 uncooked Manicotti shells
- 1 cup of ricotta cheese
- 4 ounce of cream cheese
- 1 tablespoon of dry Italian seasoning
- ¼ cup cooked and drained spinach
- 8 ounce of cooked frozen shrimp cut in half
- ¼ cup diced onion and 1 garlic clove cooked together
- 3 ounces shredded mozzarella
- ¼ cup Parmesan cheese
- 1 cup of homemade marinara sauce
- 1/2 cup of homemade pesto sauce
- Chopped parsley for garnish
- Serve with warm garlic bread

Ingredients - Pesto Sauce

- 1 cup fresh basil leaves
- 3 cloves garlic
- 3 tablespoons of pine nuts roasted lightly
- 1/3 cup Parmesan cheese
- 1/3 cup olive oil
- Salt and pepper to taste

Putting the Pesto Together

- Combine all the ingredients except oil in a food processor
- Turn on motor and slowly add the olive oil in a stream until it is emulsified
- Add addition salt and pepper to taste

Can be made up to 1 week in advance; stored in an airtight container

Ingredients - Marinara Sauce

- 2 tablespoons olive oil
- 1 small onion chopped
- 1 garlic clove minced
- 1 tablespoon sugar
- 2 teaspoons of fresh chopped basil
- 16 ounce can diced tomatoes
- 6-ounce tomato paste

Putting the Marinara Together

- In a saucepan heat olive oil and cook onion and garlic till tender
- Stir in sugar, basil, tomatoes, and tomato paste
- Heat mixture to boiling, stirring to break up tomatoes

- Reduce heat to low, cover saucepan turn down to low
- Simmer 20 minutes adjust seasoning if needed with salt and pepper

Putting It All Together

- Preheat oven to 350 degrees
- Cook manicotti as directed on package; drain and rinse in cold water
- In med bowl combine ricotta, cream cheese, spinach, shrimp, onion, garlic, mozzarella and parmesan cheese
- Mix well then stuff the filling into the cooked manicotti
- Spread ½ cup marinara sauce on the bottom of a casserole dish
- Lay the filled manicotti on top of the marinara sauce lengthwise
- Layer on top of the manicotti with one side having pesto sauce and the other side marinara sauce for the Italian flag presentation
- Sprinkle 2 tablespoons of Parmesan cheese and 1/3 cup of mozzarella
- Bake the manicotti for 30 minutes; remove from oven and let rest for 10 minutes
- Serve hot with a garnish of chopped parsley, your favorite side dish and garlic bread

Serve 2 each for 4 people for entrée or serve 1 each as an appetizer for 8 people

Southwestern Lobster Cake with Aioli Sauce

Ingredients

- 1 lb. cooked lobster coarsely chopped
- 1 cup panko breadcrumbs
- ½ small onion diced
- 1 small jalapeno finely diced
- 1 tablespoon fresh chopped cilantro
- 2 tablespoons Dijon mustard
- ½ teaspoon Lea & Perrins sauce
- 1 teaspoon fresh squeezed lemon juice
- 1 teaspoon southwestern seasoning
- Sprigs of cilantro for garnish

Ingredients - Aioli Sauce

- ¾ cup mayonnaise
- 3 tablespoons finely chopped cilantro leaves
- 1 tablespoon finely chopped garlic
- ½ teaspoon southwestern seasoning
- 1 tablespoon lemon juice

Putting the Aoili Together

- Mix all the ingredients together
- Cover in an airtight container; refrigerate until service time

Putting It All Together

- Combine all the Southwestern Lobster ingredients together; shape into 8 lobster cakes
- In a hot 12-inch skillet melt 2 tablespoons of butter
- Place cakes in pan; cook 3 to 4 minutes on each side
- Remove from pan and cover; keep warm until service
- Garnish with cilantro sprig
- Serve with Aoili Sauce on the side

Serves 8 individual cakes

Stuffed Shrimp Poblano with Tomatillo Sauce

Ingredients

- 4 large poblano split in half
- 2 tablespoons butter; melted
- 1 teaspoon ground black pepper
- ½ teaspoon salt
- 2 celery ribs chopped fine
- ½ yellow onion chopped
- 4 ounces of cream cheese at room temperature
- 4 ounces of goat cheese
- 1 pound chopped cooked and peeled shrimp
- 2 cups shredded Mexican cheese blend
- 1 teaspoon cumin
- 1 teaspoon Mexican oregano
- 2 tablespoons lemon juice
- 1 6-ounce jar tomatillo sauce
- Chopped parsley for garnish

Ingredients - Breadcrumb topping for the poblano's:

- Finely crushed 1 cup breadcrumbs and ½ cup finely crushed Frito lay chips
- Mixed together with 3 tablespoon melted butter

Putting It All Together

- Preheat oven to 350 degrees
- Cut the peppers lengthwise in ½ and discard the seeds
- Place peppers down on an ungreased sheet pan and broil for 15 minutes or until tender
- In a large pan sauté onions and celery in 2 tablespoons butter till translucent
- Add cream cheese, goat cheese, shredded Mexican cheese, shrimp, spices and lemon juice
- Fill each poblano with the filling and top with breadcrumb topping
- Place on an ungreased sheet pan and bake for 10 to 15 minutes or until golden brown
- Serve with a drizzle of tomatillo sauce and chopped parsley for garnish

Serves 4 people

Sweet Onion Tartlet

Ingredients - Tartlet

- ½ cup butter
- 3 ounces cream cheese
- 1 cup flour

Ingredients - Sweet Onion Filling

- 3 tablespoons olive oil
- 2 medium onions sliced and quartered
- 1 clove of garlic finely mashed
- 2 teaspoons of marmalade
- 2 tablespoons balsamic vinegar
- 4 tablespoons plump raisins
- ¼ cup pinon nuts
- About 3 ounces feta or goat cheese
- Chopped parsley for garnish

Putting Tartlet Together

- Preheat oven to 350 degrees
- In mixing bowl combine butter and cream cheese
- Slowly add flour and mix well
- Form into 24 - two-inch balls on miniature muffin tin and refrigerate for 15 minutes
- Use your finger to mash down the balls into tartlet shapes; bake 5 to 10 minutes
- Take tartlet shells out of muffin tin and let cool

Putting the Filling Together

- Heat oil and sauté onions and garlic on low covered until golden brown
- Increase the heat add marmalade, balsamic vinegar, and raisins
- Cook the filling until most of the liquid has evaporated
- Cool the filling and fill the tartlet shells with onion mixture and sprinkle feta or goat cheese on each tartlet
- Serve with a garnish of chopped parsley

Serves 24 appetizers

Sweet Potato and Chorizo Empanadas with Creamy Cilantro Sauce

Ingredients

- 1 cup finely diced and cooked chorizo
- 1 large cooked and finely diced sweet potato
- 1 onion
- 2 cloves garlic
- 1 tablespoon vegetable oil
- ½ teaspoon dry cumin
- ½ teaspoon Mexican oregano
- 1 box frozen puff pastry
- 1 egg slightly beaten

Putting It All Together

- Preheat Oven to 350 degrees
- Sauté onions and garlic in oil until translucent
- Add the chorizo, sweet potato and spices to the onions and garlic mixture
- Cook until all is incorporated for about 5 minutes; let mixture cool
- Use a 5-inch cookie cutter on the puff pastry; brush each cut out pastry with egg wash on the edges and fill with 1 teaspoon of mixture in the middle
- Fold the pastry in half; seal edges with a fork and lay onto a silicone sheet pan
- Brush top of each empanada with remaining egg wash and bake in for 20 min.

Ingredients - Creamy Cilantro Sauce

- 1 cup Cilantro leaves and stems
- ¼ cup plain Greek Yogurt
- ¼ cup sour cream
- 2 minced garlic cloves
- 4 tablespoons lemon juice
- 4 tablespoons olive oil
- ¼ teaspoon cumin
- 1 medium Jalapeno deseeded and chopped fine
- Salt and pepper to taste

Putting It All Together

- Mix all ingredients in food processor; blend until smooth; store in airtight container
- Serve warm with a side of creamy cilantro sauce

Serves 24 appetizers

Thai Shrimp Cakes with Jalapeno Sauce

Ingredients

- 1 lb. med shrimp peeled, deveined and chopped
- 1 ½ cup panko breadcrumbs
- ½ cup finely diced green bell pepper
- ½ cup finely diced yellow onion
- ¼ cup chopped fresh cilantro
- 4 teaspoons lime juice
- 2 teaspoons fish sauce
- 2 teaspoons sweet chili sauce
- 2 large eggs well beaten
- 2 garlic cloves minced
- 2 tablespoons olive oil for sautéing the cakes

Ingredients - Jalapeno Plum Sauce

- 1 ½ tablespoon vegetable oil
- ½ cup honey
- ¼ cup red onion
- 1/3 cup lemon juice
- 2 tablespoons finely chopped jalapeno pepper
- 3 tablespoons soy sauce
- 3 cups of unpeeled plums
- 1 ½ teaspoons all spice
- 1 ½ tablespoons minced garlic
- 1 ½ teaspoons curry

Putting the Sauce Together

- Sauté onion, jalapeno and garlic in oil till tender
- Add the remaining ingredients and cook uncovered for 30 minutes

Putting It All Together

- Combine all the ingredients together and shape into 4 even cakes
- Sauté in a hot skillet with olive oil until golden brown on each side
- Serve Jalapeno Sauce warm on the side or on plate with the cakes

Serves 4 people

Soups . . .

- ❖ Apple Butternut Bisque Soup with Roasted Chestnuts
- ❖ Avocado and Crab Soup
- ❖ Boston Fish Chowder
- ❖ Carrot Ginger Soup
- ❖ Coconut Curry Lentil Soup
- ❖ Cream Artichoke Saffron Soup
- ❖ Cream of Avocado & Creamy Black Bean Soup
- ❖ Cream of Celeriac Soup
- ❖ Cream of Chicken Alfredo Soup
- ❖ Cream of Fennel Soup
- ❖ Creamy Louisiana Crawfish Bisque
- ❖ Old English Scallop Chowder
- ❖ Peruvian Potato Soup
- ❖ Pumpkin and Sage Soup
- ❖ Pumpkin Apple Bisque Soup
- ❖ Roasted Acorn Squash and Pear Soup
- ❖ Roasted Garlic and Spinach Soup
- ❖ Senegalese Soup
- ❖ Spicy Cream Corn Soup
- ❖ Waterzooi Soup
- ❖ Wild Mushroom Soup

For Any Occasion Homemade Stock:

- ❖ Homemade Beef Stock
- ❖ Homemade Chicken Stock
- ❖ Homemade Seafood Stock

Apple Butternut Bisque with Roasted Chestnuts

Ingredients

- 1 Butternut squash (3 lbs.)
- 1 tablespoon olive oil
- 3 Macintosh apples peeled and diced
- 1 large onion
- 2 medium carrots peeled and diced
- ½ teaspoon cinnamon
- ¼ teaspoon nutmeg
- 3 tablespoons honey (optional)
- 5 cups vegetable stock
- 1 cup heavy cream
- 2 tablespoons chop fresh parsley
- ½ cup roasted chestnuts (canned)
- Salt and pepper to taste

Putting It All Together

- Preheat oven to 400 degrees
- Split the butternut squash in half and clean out seeds, drizzle with olive oil
- Bake for about 1 hour
- Take out of oven and let cool then remove the pulp
- In a Dutch oven sauté onions, carrots, and apple until tender
- Add the spices, butternut squash and vegetable stock, simmer for 15 minutes
- Puree the soup with an immersion or regular blender and slowly add cream, adjust taste with salt and pepper
- Garnish with roasted chestnuts and parsley

Serves 6 to 8 people

Avocado and Crab Soup

Ingredients

- 1 cup of fresh lump crabmeat
- 2 ribs celery stalk diced
- 1 tablespoon fresh chopped chive
- 1 teaspoon grated lemon zest
- 2 ripe avocados
- 2 cups of vegetable stock
- 1/2 cup sour cream
- 2 tablespoons lime juice
- Salt and pepper to taste
- Chopped chives for garnish
- ½ cup diced croutons for garnish

Putting It All Together

- Mix the crabmeat, celery, chive and lemon in a bowl, cover
- Cut the avocados in half and remove the meat
- Put into a blender adding the vegetable stock, sour cream lime juice with any salt and pepper
- Puree until smooth, if too thick add a bit of water
- Add the crabmeat mixture to the soup and chill until service time
- Garnish with croutons and chop chives

Serves 4 people

Boston Fish Soup

Ingredients

- 2 pounds of fish fillets, (Fresh or Frozen perch cod or flounder)
- 6 slices thick bacon
- ½ cup chopped onion
- ½ cup chopped celery
- 2 garlic cloves minced
- ½ teaspoon each of rosemary, thyme and parsley
- 1 bay leaf
- ½ cup all-purpose flour
- 5 cups seafood stock
- 2 russet potatoes peeled, cubed into small bites and par cook set aside
- 2 cups half and half cream
- Serve with oyster crackers – approximately 1 cup
- Optional bread bowls

Putting It All Together

- In a Dutch oven cook bacon until crisp, remove and set aside leaving the bacon grease
- Add the onions, garlic, celery and sauté until tender
- Add the herbs stir in the flour and slowly add the seafood stock until smooth
- Add the cooked potatoes and bacon along with the fresh or frozen fish and cook for 15 minutes
- Add the cream at the end and serve hot either in a traditional bowl or bread bowl with oyster crackers

Serves 6 to 8 people

Carrot Ginger Soup

Ingredients

- 2 tablespoons olive oil
- 1 cup chopped yellow onions
- 2 garlic cloves minced
- 5 carrots peeled and chopped
- 2 teaspoons fresh ginger
- 2 tablespoons apple cider vinegar
- 3 cups vegetable stock
- 1 cup apple sauce
- 1 cup coconut milk
- Salt and pepper to taste
- 2 tablespoons of chop parsley for garnish
- 1 cup diced and toasted croutons for garnish

Putting It All Together

- Heat oil in a large pot over medium heat
- Add the onions and garlic, sauté until tender
- Add carrots ginger, apple cider and vegetable stock cooking until carrots are soft
- Put everything into a blender and puree until smooth, add the coconut last
- Taste the soup for desired flavor, add salt and pepper as needed
- Serve hot or cold with a toasted croutons and parsley

Serves 6 to 8 people (1 cup serving each)

Coconut Curry Lentil Soup

Ingredients

- 2 cups dry brown lentils
- 2 tablespoons coconut oil
- 1 cup diced onion
- 1 each carrot and celery diced
- 2 cloves garlic minced
- ½ small jalapeno pepper seeded and diced
- 2 teaspoons dry ginger
- 1 teaspoon curry powder
- 2 russet potatoes peeled and diced
- 4 cups chicken stock
- 1 can coconut milk
- Salt and pepper to taste
- ¼ cup chopped peanuts for garnish
- 3 tablespoons chopped parsley for garnish
- ½ cup toasted coconut for garnish

Putting It All Together

- In a large stock pot on medium heat sauté in coconut oil the onions, garlic, carrot, celery, and jalapeno until tender
- Add the spices and cook for 5 more minutes, then add chicken stock, coconut milk, diced potatoes and lentils for another 20 minutes
- Move everything into a blender and puree until smooth
- Serve with shredded toasted coconut, chopped peanuts, and parsley

Serves 6 people (1 cup each)

Cream Artichoke Saffron Soup Topped with Fried Onions

Ingredients

- 3 tablespoons olive oil
- 2 garlic cloves minced
- 1 medium onion diced
- 2 ribs celery chopped
- 1 (15 ounce) can artichoke, drained
- 4 cups chicken stock
- ¼ teaspoon saffron
- 1 cup heavy cream
- Salt and pepper to taste
- Crispy canned fried onions for garnish (2 teaspoons each)

Putting It All Together

- Heat the olive oil in a pot on medium
- Add onions, garlic, and celery and sauté until tender
- Add artichoke and chicken stock along with saffron, cook for 20 minutes,
- Move everything into a blender and puree until smooth
- Add heavy cream and adjust taste with salt and pepper
- Top with your favorite crispy canned fried onions

Serves 6 people

Cream of Avocado & Creamy Black Bean Soup

Ingredients - Cream of Avocado Soup

- 3 tablespoons olive oil
- 2 cloves of garlic
- 1 small onion
- 2 medium russet potatoes peeled and cubed
- 3 cups chicken stock
- 2 large avocados
- 1 cup heavy cream
- ¼ cup sour cream for garnish
- 1 tablespoon chopped fresh parsley
- Salt and Pepper to taste

Putting It All Together

- In a Dutch oven heat olive oil over medium
- Add onion and garlic, sauté until tender
- Add chicken stock and potatoes, simmer for 15 minutes
- Pour soup in a blender with the avocados and puree until smooth
- Chill soup, then add heavy cream, salt and pepper to taste

Ingredients - Creamy Black Bean Soup

- 3 tablespoons olive oil
- 1 medium onion diced
- 2 garlic cloves minced
- 1 jalapeno seeded and diced
- 1 (4 ounce) can green chili
- 1 (15 ounce) diced tomatoes
- 2 (15 ounce) cans black beans with juice
- 1 teaspoon chili powder
- 1 teaspoon dry cumin powder
- 4 cups chicken stock
- 1 lime cut into 6 wedges
- ¼ cup sour cream to drizzle lightly atop soup

Putting It All Together

- In a Dutch oven sauté in hot oil: onions, garlic and jalapeno until tender-3-4 min.
- Add the black beans, tomatoes and spices and cook for about 5 minutes
- Add the chicken stock and simmer for another 20 minutes
- Put everything into a blender and puree until smooth
- Top with a drizzled sour cream, serve side of lime wedge

Marrying the Soups Together

- Put each soup into separate pitchers and simultaneously pour them into a flat bowl evenly so half of the bowl is black bean and the other half is avocado
- Then drizzle sour cream in the middle

Serves 4-6people in wide soup bowls

Cream of Celeriac Soup

Ingredients

- 3 tablespoons olive oil
- 1 medium size celeriac peeled and diced
- 1 leek washed and diced
- 1 large russet potato peeled and diced
- 1 medium size yellow onion chopped
- 2 garlic cloves minced
- 4 cups chicken stock
- 1 cup heavy cream
- ½ cup dark rye toasted croutons for garnish
- 2 tablespoons fresh chop chive for garnish
- Salt and Pepper to taste

Putting It All Together

- In a medium pot heat olive oil and sauté the onions, garlic, celeriac, leek and potatoes until the celeriac is tender (about 10 minutes)
- Add the vegetables in the same pot with chicken stock and cook for 20 minutes
- Put everything into a blender and puree until smooth
- Return the blended soup into the soup pot and add in the heavy cream
- Serve with toasted dark rye croutons and chopped chives
- Adjust with salt and pepper to taste

Serves 4-6people

Cream of Chicken Alfredo and Tortellini Soup

Ingredients

- 3 tablespoons olive oil
- 3 tablespoons butter
- 2 chicken breasts (8 ounce each)
- 1 yellow onion diced
- 4 garlic cloves minced
- 1 teaspoon red pepper flakes
- ½ cup all-purpose flour
- 1 cup parmesan cheese
- 1 cup heavy cream
- Small package of tortellini
- Salt and pepper to taste
- ¼ cup chopped parsley
- ¼ cup parmesan cheese for garnish (divided)

Putting It All Together

- Cook chicken in olive oil and butter for 5 minutes on each side and set aside
- Add the onions, garlic, and red pepper flakes, sauté until soft
- Add the flour and stir until it is incorporated making a roux
- Add chicken stock to the roux stirring until it becomes a smooth sauce
- Add the parmesan cheese and diced chicken breast to the soup
- Cook tortellini according to package then add it to the soup
- To finish, add the heavy cream and stir lightly
- Garnish the top with chopped parsley and parmesan cheese

Serves 4-6 people

Cream of Fennel Soup

Ingredients

- 4 tablespoons butter
- 3 Fennel bulbs
- 1 large onion diced
- 1 leek washed and diced
- 3 medium russet potatoes peeled and diced
- 6 cups chicken stock
- 1 cup heavy cream
- 1 cup diced and toasted croutons for garnish
- ¼ cup chopped fresh chives for garnish (divided)
- Salt and pepper to taste

Putting It All Together

- Melt butter in a Dutch oven on medium heat, sauté fennel until tender
- Stir in onions and leeks and sauté for 3 to 5 minutes
- Add peeled potatoes and chicken stock
- Bring to boil then reduce heat and cook for 15 minutes
- Put the stock into a blender and puree until smooth
- Stir in the heavy cream and adjust the taste with salt and pepper
- Garnish with croutons and chop fresh chives

(Can be served hot or cold)

Serves 6 - 8 people (1 cup serving)

Creamy Louisiana Crawfish Bisque

Ingredients

- 4 tablespoons butter
- 4 tablespoons flour
- 1 small onion diced
- 2 garlic cloves
- 1 cup heavy cream
- 1 each of red and green pepper, seeded and diced
- 1 Jalapeno seeded and diced
- 4 tablespoons tomato paste
- 5 cups seafood stock
- 1-pound crawfish tails
- 3 teaspoons creole seasoning
- Louisiana hot sauce to taste
- 1/3 cup scallion sliced diagonal
- 1 cup dice and toasted croutons for garnish

Putting It All Together

- Heat butter in Dutch oven on medium, add onion, garlic, peppers and jalapeno until tender
- Add flour and stir for about 2 minutes then add tomato paste and stir for another 1 to 2 minutes
- Add the seasoning and seafood stock, slowly stirring to avoid lumps
- Bring to a boil and reduce heat to a simmer for about 10 minutes
- Add everything in a blender and puree until smooth
- Adjust the taste with salt, pepper and hot sauce
- Add heavy cream then the crawfish to finish the soup.
- Garnish with croutons

Serves 6 - 8 people (1 cup serving)

Old English Scallop Chowder

Ingredients

- 4 slices of bacon chopped
- ½ onion diced
- 1 clove garlic minced
- 3 ribs of celery diced
- 2 carrots peeled and diced
- 1 small green bell pepper diced
- 1 tablespoon dry thyme
- 4 tablespoons butter
- 4 tablespoons flour
- 5 cups of seafood
- 1 bay leaf
- 1 russet potato peeled and diced in small cubes
- 1 pound of bay scallops
- ½ teaspoon hot sauce
- ½ cup heavy cream salt and pepper to taste
- Oyster crackers for garnish (approximately 1 cup divided)

Putting It All Together

- Sauté bacon over medium heat until it begins to brown, about 3 minutes
- Add onion, garlic, celery and carrots until tender
- Add the melted butter and flour until it comes together
- Mix in the seafood stock and whisk until the soup thickens
- Add bay leaf and bring to a simmer
- Add the diced potato and cook for 10 minutes
- Add the scallops, hot sauce, salt and pepper, cook for 5 minutes longer and finish off with heavy cream
- Serve hot with oyster crackers

Serves 6 - 8 people (1 cup serving)

Peruvian Potato Soup

Ingredients

- 4 tablespoons butter
- 1 large leek cleaned and chopped
- 1 medium onion chopped
- 2 garlic cloves chopped
- 2 pounds of purple potatoes quartered
- 5 cups vegetable stock
- 1 cup half and half cream
- 2 tablespoons chopped fresh chives for garnish
- Garlic bread

Putting It All Together

- In a Dutch oven sauté the onions, leek and garlic together in butter
- Add the vegetable stock along with the purple potatoes and cook until the potatoes are fork tender
- Blend the soup in a blender until smooth
- Chill the soup and add cream
- Garnish with chives on top of soup
- Serve with side of garlic bread

Serves 6 - 8 people (1 cup serving)

Pumpkin and Sage Soup

Ingredients

- ¼ cup olive oil
- 3 medium yellow onions
- 3 garlic cloves minced
- 3 fresh sage leaves
- 1 tablespoon fresh grated ginger
- ¼ teaspoon nutmeg
- 4 cups chicken stock
- 2 (15ounce) cans of pumpkin
- 1 cup heavy cream
- ½ cup toasted pumpkin seeds for garnish
- 2 tablespoons chop fresh parsley for garnish
- Salt and pepper to taste

Putting It All Together

- In a medium stock pot heat oil and add onions and garlic, sauté until translucent
- Add the fresh sage leaves, ginger, nutmeg and chicken stock, cook for 5 minutes
- Add pumpkin and cook for another 20 minutes
- Blend everything into a blender then let cool
- Once cool add heavy cream and chill
- Top the cold soup with toasted pumpkin seeds and parsley

Serves 4-6 people

Pumpkin Apple Bisque

Ingredients

- 1 tablespoon butter
- 1 small onion chopped
- 1 tablespoon ginger grated
- 1 (15 ounce) can pumpkin puree
- 1 (14 ½ ounce) can apple sauce
- 2 cups chicken stock
- 2 tablespoons honey
- 1 teaspoon apple cider vinegar
- 1 cinnamon stick
- ¼ teaspoon nutmeg
- ¾ cup sour cream
- ½ cup diced and dehydrated chopped apple for garnish
- ¼ cup chopped parsley for garnish
- Salt and pepper to taste

Putting It All Together

- Melt butter over medium heat in a large saucepan,
- Sauté the onions and ginger until onions are tender
- Add pumpkin, apple sauce, chicken stock, honey, vinegar, cinnamon stick and nutmeg, then simmer for 20 minutes
- Let chill then stir in sour cream and top with dehydrated diced apple and parsley

Serves 6 people

Roasted Acorn Squash and Pear Soup

Ingredients

- 3 tablespoons olive oil
- 3 tablespoons butter
- 2 medium acorn squash peeled and diced
- 4 Bartlett pears peeled and diced
- 3 celery ribs diced
- 1 yellow onion
- 2 teaspoons dry thyme
- 4 cups chicken stock
- 1 cup heavy cream
- 1 cup diced and toasted croutons for garnish
- ¼ cup chopped parsley for garnish
- Salt and pepper to taste

Putting It All Together

- Preheat oven to 350 degrees
- Drizzle the vegetables with olive oil, butter and thyme then lay onto a parchment lined tray and roast for 1 hour or until tender
- Put the roasted vegetables in a pot with the chicken stock and cook for 10 minutes
- Put the stock into a blender and puree until smooth then add cream
- Adjust the soup with salt and pepper to taste
- Garnish the soup with croutons and chopped parsley

Serves 6 people

Roasted Garlic and Spinach Soup

Ingredients

- 1 medium yellow onion chopped
- 5 garlic cloves peeled and diced
- 2 carrots peeled and chopped
- 3 to 4 tablespoons olive oil
- 2 cups of chicken or vegetable stock (Homemade preferred)
- ¼ cup fresh basil
- 1 cup heavy cream
- 1 cup fried onions (can or homemade) for garnish
- Salt and Pepper to taste
- Optional to serve with diced/cooked chicken

Putting It All Together

- Preheat oven to 400 degrees
- Toss the onions, garlic, and carrots in olive oil and roast for 30 minutes
- Meanwhile heat chicken stock and add the spinach until it has wilted down in the stock
- Take the roasted vegetables, basil and spinach in the chicken stock and blend it in a food processor or blender until smooth
- Add heavy cream, adjust taste with salt and pepper
- Top the soup with fried onions that are homemade or from a can

(You can also add diced chicken that has been poached or grilled)

Serves 4-6 people

Senegalese Soup

Ingredients

- 3 Granny Smith apples peeled and diced
- 2 tablespoons unsalted butter
- 2 carrots chopped
- 2 ribs celery chopped
- 1 large onion chopped
- 1 garlic clove minced
- 3 tablespoons curry powder
- 2 tablespoons all-purpose flour
- 8 cups chicken broth
- 1 tablespoon can tomato puree
- ½ cup heavy cream
- Garnish with 1 teaspoon each of toasted coconut, chopped peanuts, chutney or diced apples
- Pita bread or croutons for garnish

Putting It All Together

- In a heavy saucepan heat butter over moderate heat
- Add apples, carrots, celery, onions and garlic, stirring now and then until everything is soft
- Add flour and curry powder, cook for 1 minute
- Stir in chicken broth and tomato puree, simmer on low for about an hour then add cream
- Salt and pepper to taste, garnish with toasted coconut, chopped peanuts, chutney or diced apples
- Serve hot with toasted pita bread or any other bread or croutons

Serves 8 people

Spicy Cream Corn Soup

Ingredients

- 2 cans (15 ounce) corn drained
- 1 can (13.5 ounce) coconut milk
- 1 Yellow onion diced
- 2 garlic cloves minced
- 3 tablespoons olive oil
- 1 small jalapeno seeded and diced
- 4 cups chicken stock
- 1 cup cream
- ¼ cup chopped parsley for garnish (divided)
- Salt and pepper to taste

Putting It All Together

- Sauté onions, garlic, and jalapeno until tender
- Add corn and chicken stock and cook for 20 minutes
- Put everything into a blender and puree until smooth
- Add cream and adjust with salt and pepper to taste
- Garnish with chopped parsley

Serves 4-6 people

Waterzooi Soup (Cream of Chicken Soup)

Ingredients

- 4 tablespoons butter
- 2 carrots peeled and diced small
- 2 ribs celery finely diced small
- 1 medium onion diced small
- 1 leek washed and diced small
- 1 cup russet potato peeled and diced small
- 4 tablespoons all-purpose flour
- 6 cups chicken stock
- 4 boneless chicken breasts cooked and diced small
- 1 cup heavy cream
- 2 large egg yolks
- 1 tablespoon fresh chopped chives or parsley for garnish (divided)
- Baguette (warmed)
- Salt and Pepper to taste

Putting It All Together

- Add butter to a stock pot along with the vegetables and cook until soft
- Add flour to the vegetables and stir until it is mixed well
- Add chicken stock and bring to boil, then reduce heat and
- Add chicken breast in stock, poach the chicken for 10 minutes
- Remove chicken from pot and set aside in a bowl to cool
- Once chicken is cool dice in small pieces and return it to the pot
- Whisk together the cream and egg yolk in a clean bowl and slowly fold into the stock
- Serve warm topped with chopped chive or parsley and warm baguette

Serves 6 to 8 people

Wild Mushroom Soup

Ingredients

- 3 tablespoons butter
- 3 tablespoons olive oil
- ¼ cup flour
- 1 medium yellow onion
- 4 garlic cloves minced
- 1-pound assorted fresh mushrooms
- 2 tablespoons fresh thyme
- 4 tablespoons dry sherry
- 5 cups chicken stock
- 1 cup heavy cream
- Fresh parsley (chopped) for garnish
- Puff pastry crouton (garnish top)
- Salt and pepper to taste

Putting It All Together

- Melt butter and olive oil into a large pot on medium heat
- Add onions and garlic, sauté until tender
- Add mushrooms making sure you discard the stem from any shiitakes
- Add thyme and sauté until the mushrooms are cooked through
- Deglaze with the sherry, then add flour making a roux
- Stir in the chicken stock until the soup thickens
- Puree the soup in a blender until smooth
- Add heavy cream and adjust taste with salt and pepper
- Garnish the top with a puff pastry crouton and chopped fresh parsley

Serves 6 people

Homemade Beef Stock

Ingredients

- 6 pounds of beef bones and trimmings
- 2 onions chopped with peelings quartered
- 2 large carrots cut into 2-inch pieces
- 3 ribs of celery cut into 2-inch pieces
- 1 parsnip cut into 2-inch pieces
- 4 to 5 sprigs of thyme and parsley
- 2 bay leaves
- 1 tablespoon peppercorn
- 3 to 4 tablespoons olive oil
- 3 tablespoons tomato paste
- 4 quarts of water

Putting It All Together

- Preheat oven to 400 degrees
- Cut the bones into 1-inch pieces and put in a large pot
- Add the vegetables and mix with the olive oil
- Bake in the oven for 45 minutes tossing occasionally so that the beef browns evenly
- Remove the beef bones and vegetables from the stockpot and set aside
- Pour off any excess grease and put stock pot on stove
- Add tomato paste and cook for 2 minutes, add 2 cups of the water and bring to simmer
- Add the bones and vegetables back into the stock pot and add remaining 3 quarts of cold water
- Bring the stock pot to a boil then reduce heat to simmer for 3 to 4 hours
- Occasionally skim off any foam scum from the top
- Strain the stock through a cheese cloth, then cover and chill in the refrigerator
- Once chilled remove the solid fat from the surface
- Put the stock into airtight containers or jars to freeze making sure to mark and date the containers for freshness

Yields roughly 8 to 10 cups

Homemade Chicken Stock

Ingredients

- 2 whole chicken carcasses
- 1 onion
- 3 carrots
- 3 celery stalks
- 2 sprigs of rosemary and thyme
- 2 bay leaves
- 1 tablespoon black peppercorns
- 2 teaspoons salt
- 8 to 10 cups cold water

Putting It All Together

- Cut the onions, carrots, and celery in 1-inch pieces
- Place the carcasses into a pot filled with 8 to 10 cups of cold water (enough to cover)
- Add the vegetables, fresh herbs, bay leaves, peppercorns and salt
- Bring the stock to a boil and reduce heat to simmer, cook for 3 to 4 hours (chicken should be tender)
- Strain the broth threw a strainer, then discard the bones and vegetables
- Let broth cool, then refrigerate or freeze
- If you plan to freeze, make sure to mark and date the containers for freshness

Yields 8 - 10 cups

Homemade Seafood Stock

Ingredients

- 2 tablespoons olive oil
- 1 whole onion diced
- 3 whole carrots
- 4 stocks of celery
- 5 cloves garlic peeled
- 2 pounds fish bones and heads
- 3 cups water
- 3 cups dry white wine
- Couple slices of lemon
- 2 bay leaves
- 6 sprigs of each fresh thyme and parsley
- 1 teaspoon fennel seeds
- 6 crushed peppercorns
- Salt to taste

Putting It All Together

- Wash fish well and remove gills from heads
- Combine in a pan with all the other ingredients except salt.
- Bring to a boil then reduce heat to simmer for 20 to 30 minutes
- Taste and add salt if needed
- Cool and strain stock then refrigerate or freeze
- Mark, label and date the stock for freshness

Serves 6 people (1 cup serving)

Salads . . .

- ❖ Arizona Cactus Salad with Honey Lime Vinaigrette
- ❖ Arugula and Watercress Salad
- ❖ Asian Salad with Oriental Vinaigrette
- ❖ Asian Carrot Slaw in Waffle Bowl
- ❖ Celeriac and Radish Salad with Louis Dressing
- ❖ Farro and Roasted Eggplant Salad
- ❖ Hawaiian Tropical Carrot and Coconut Salad
- ❖ Hearts of Palm Salad with Maltese Sauce
- ❖ Jicama, Walnut, Apple, Fig Salad with Thai Dressing
- ❖ Lentil and Cucumber Salad with Feta Cheese
- ❖ Kimchi Noodle Salad on Rice Cake Bowl
- ❖ Mango, Avocado and Goat Cheese with Mango Vinaigrette
- ❖ Poached Pear Stuffed Gorgonzola with Champagne Dressing
- ❖ Pomegranate and Persimmon Salad
- ❖ Red and Yellow Roasted Beet Salad with Pistachio and Goat Cheese
- ❖ Watercress, Radish and Onion Salad with Poppyseed Vinaigrette

Arizona Cactus Salad

Ingredients - Salad

- 1 Jar (15-ounce) Nopalitos drained and rinsed
- 1 can (15-ounce) yellow hominy drained
- 3 Roma tomatoes diced
- 1 red onion diced
- 2 avocados diced
- ½ cup chopped cilantro
- 1 lime (juiced)
- 1 tablespoon dry oregano
- ¼ cup crumbled Queso Fresco cheese
- 4 Flour tortillas bowls (from the grocery store)

Ingredients - Honey Lime Vinaigrette

- ¼ cup fresh lime juice
- 2 tablespoons honey
- 1 teaspoon sugar
- 1 teaspoon Dijon mustard
- ½ teaspoon garlic powder
- ¼ teaspoon dry cumin
- ¼ teaspoon Mexican oregano
- ½ cup canola oil
- Salt and pepper to taste

Putting It Vinaigrette Together

- Puree the lime juice, honey, sugar, mustard, garlic powder, and cumin in a blender
- Pour the oil slowly into the blender while mixing to emulsify into the dressing.
- Once mixed evenly adjust the taste with salt and pepper and keep refrigerated until ready to use
- Shake the dressing mixture well before use

Putting It All Together

- Slice the Nopalitos make sure they are rinsed well and not slimy
- In a large bowl add the Nopalitos, yellow hominy, diced Roma tomatoes, red onion and avocado, chopped cilantro, oregano, and juice of one lime
- Toss all together in the bowl and place the ingredients into a baked flour tortilla bowl and add crumbled Queso Fresco cheese to the top of the salad and drizzle with dressing

Serves 4 people

Arugula and Watercress Salad with Honey Poppyseed Dressing

Ingredients

- 3 cups arugula
- 3 cups watercress
- ½ cup sliced radishes
- ½ cup sliced red onion
- ½ cup toasted pine nuts
- ½ cup crumbled goat cheese

Ingredients - Honey Poppyseed Dressing

- ½ cup olive oil
- 3 teaspoons honey
- 3 teaspoons apple cider vinegar
- 2 teaspoons poppyseed
- Salt and pepper to taste

Putting It All Together

- Mix the dressing ingredients in a bowl or vessel of your choice and refrigerate until service time
- Wash the lettuce under cold water and drain well
- Mix all the salad ingredients together in a bowl
- Drizzle the dressing lightly over the salad just before service time

Serves 4 people

Asian Carrot Slaw Salad in Waffle Bowl

Ingredients - Slaw

- 5 carrots peeled and shredded
- ½ red onion shredded
- 1 cup shredded Napa cabbage
- 3 scallions cut diagonally
- Toasted sesame seeds for garnish
- Sliced scallions for garnish

Ingredients - Asian Dressing

- ½ cup rice vinegar
- ¼ cup sugar
- ½ cup Thai sweet chili sauce
- 2 tablespoons chopped mint

Ingredients - Waffle Bowl Batter

- 2/3 cup all-purpose flour
- ¼ teaspoon salt
- 2 eggs room temperature
- 2 tablespoons sugar
- 4 tablespoons melted butter
- ¼ cup whole milk

Putting It All Together

- Heat your waffle cone maker ahead of time
- Mix all the waffle ingredients together and refrigerate for about 15 minutes
- Spray the waffle cone maker with cooking spray and pour ¼ of batter into the waffle maker
- Refer to your cone maker's instructions for cook time
- Lay the waffles over an inverted bowl to form
- Prepare salad by combining carrots, red onion, Napa cabbage, and scallions
- Prepare Asian vinaigrette dressing by combining, rice vinegar, sugar, Thai sweet chili sauce, and chopped mint
- Toss the salad ingredients with Asian dressing
- Load the salad into the waffle bowls as desired
- Top with toasted sesame seeds and scallions

Serves 4 people

Asian Vinaigrette Salad

Ingredients

- 2 celery stalks cut diagonally
- 2 carrots peeled cut in half and cut diagonally
- 1 (4 ounce) can sliced water chestnuts
- ½ red onion sliced
- 4 scallions cut diagonally
- ½ red bell pepper cut into matchsticks
- ½ cup fresh cilantro leaves (no stem)
- Toasted sesame seeds for garnish

Ingredients - Vinaigrette

- 1 tablespoon grated fresh ginger
- ¼ cup smooth peanut butter
- ¼ cup rice vinegar
- 3 tablespoons sesame oil
- 2 tablespoons water
- 1 teaspoon chili paste
- 1 garlic clove minced fine
- Salt and pepper to taste

Combine all the above ingredients and refrigerate until service time.

Putting It All Together

- Mix all the salad ingredients together in a bowl and drizzle lightly with the dressing and top with toasted sesame seeds

Serves 4 people

Celeriac and Radish Salad with Louis Dressing

Ingredients

- 1 medium celeriac root peeled and cut into small 2-inch-long matchsticks
- 6 to 8 radishes cut into small matchsticks
- 3 celery ribs cut thin diagonally
- ½ cup sliced thin red onion
- ½ cup flat leaf parsley
- ½ head iceberg lettuce shredded thin
- Garlic bread

Ingredients - Louis Dressing

- 1 cup mayonnaise
- ½ cup ketchup
- ¼ cup pickle relish
- 1 tablespoon lemon juice
- 1 teaspoon hot sauce
- ½ teaspoon each celery salt, salt and pepper

Combine all the above ingredients and refrigerate until service time.

Putting It All Together

- Combine celeriac root, radishes, celery, red onion, and parsley
- Place even amounts of the shredded lettuce on plates then divide the mixture atop
- Lightly drizzle Louis dressing over salad and serve with garlic bread

Serves 4 people

Farro and Roasted Eggplant Salad

Ingredients

- 1 cup dry Farro
- 3 cups chicken stock
- 1 bay leaf
- 1 eggplant diced
- 1 can chickpeas drained
- 1 teaspoon garlic powder
- 2 teaspoons Italian seasoning
- 4 tablespoons olive oil
- 2 Roma tomatoes seeded and diced
- ½ cup red onion diced
- ¼ cup kalamata pitted and sliced
- ½ cup toasted pine nuts
- 3 tablespoons fresh mint chopped
- Salt and pepper to taste
- Chopped parsley for garnish

Ingredients - Balsamic Vinaigrette

- 1 tablespoon honey
- 1 teaspoon Dijon mustard
- ¼ teaspoon sea salt
- ¼ teaspoon black pepper
- 1 clove garlic minced
- 2 tablespoons Balsamic
- ½ cup olive oil
- 1 head of bib lettuce for serving plates

Whisk the dressing together until combined evenly.

Putting It All Together

- Preheat oven to 350 degrees
- Boil farro in a stockpot covered in the chicken stock and bay leaf for 20-25 min.
- Drain the farro and let cool
- Place eggplant, chickpeas, seasoning on a baking sheet and drizzle with olive oil
- Roast in the oven for 35 minutes then remove and let cool
- Mix all ingredients in a bowl and drizzle lightly with Balsamic Vinaigrette
- Add mixture to a bed of bib lettuce and sprinkle with fresh chopped parsley

Serves 4 people

Hawaiian Tropical Carrot and Coconut Salad

Ingredients - Salad

- 1 (8 ounce) can crushed pineapple reserving juice
- 2 cups peeled and shredded carrots
- ½ cup toasted almonds
- ½ cup raisins soaked in rum and drained
- 1/3 cup mayonnaise
- ¼ cup pineapple juice
- 1 tablespoon coconut sugar
- ¼ teaspoon cinnamon (optional)
- ¼ cup scallions cut diagonal for garnish

Ingredients - Waffle bowl batter

- 2/3 cup all-purpose flour
- ¼ teaspoon salt
- 2 eggs room temperature
- 2 tablespoons sugar
- 4 tablespoons melted butter
- ¼ cup whole milk

Combine all the above ingredients.

Putting It All Together

- Heat your waffle cone maker ahead of time
- Mix all the waffle ingredients together and refrigerate for about 15 minutes
- Spray the waffle cone maker with cooking spray and pour ¼ of batter into the waffle maker
- Refer to your cone maker's instructions for cook time
- Lay the waffles over an inverted bowl to form
- Mix all the salad ingredients in a bowl
- Load the salad into the waffle bowls as desired
- Drizzle the dressing lightly over the salad just before service time and top with scallions

Serves 4 people

Hearts of Palm Salad with Maltese Sauce

Ingredients

- 2 (14 ounce) can hearts of palm drained
- ½ small red onion diced
- 2 avocados diced into small pieces
- Salt and pepper to taste
- ¼ cup chopped flat leaf parsley for garnish
- 1 head of bib or red leaf lettuce split 4 ways

Ingredients - Maltese Sauce

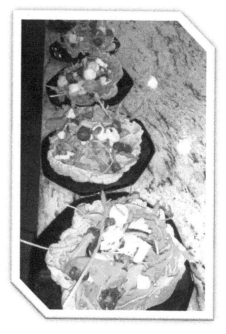

- 1 tablespoon orange juice
- 1 teaspoon orange zest
- 3 egg yolks
- 1 stick melted butter
- Dash of tabasco

Putting Sauce Together

- Put the egg yolks, salt, tabasco, orange juice and zest in a small pan over low heat
- Beat with a wire whisk until the eggs and seasoning are well blended and the egg yolks have thickened to the consistency of heavy cream
- Drizzle the butter slowly until the eggs have absorbed it all
- Keep the sauce warm on the side until ready to use.

Putting It All Together

- Cut the hearts of palm into ½ in pieces
- Combine hearts of palm, red onion, avocados and salt and pepper to taste
- Lay the salad on a bed of bib or red leaf lettuce and top with the Maltese Sauce
- Add a sprinkle of the chopped parsley on top and grind a little bit of fresh pepper, serve cold

Serves 4 people

Jicama, Walnut, Apple, Fig Salad with Thai Dressing

Ingredients

- 1 medium jicama peeled and sliced thin into matchsticks
- ½ cup walnuts chopped
- 2 Granny Smith apples peeled and sliced thin into matchsticks
- ¾ cup mission figs cut into quarters
- Chinese Napa cabbage
- Sesame seeds for garnish

Ingredients - Thai Dressing

- 1/3 cup rice wine vinegar
- 1 tablespoon fresh basil chopped
- 2 teaspoons lime juice
- 1 tablespoon fresh mint chopped
- 2 tablespoons honey
- 1 tablespoon fresh cilantro chop
- 1 teaspoon grated ginger
- ¼ teaspoon each salt and pepper
- 1 teaspoon garlic minced
- 1 tablespoon sesame oil
- ½ cup peanut oil

Combine all ingredients in a jar and shake to finish.

Putting It All Together

- Take the jicama, walnuts, apples and figs and place on top of cabbage
- Before you put the dressing on make sure you shake the dressing in a jar vigorously to combine
- Lightly drizzle the dressing over the salad and top with sesame seeds
- Serve with bread sticks

Serves 4 people

Lentil and Cucumber Salad with Feta Cheese

Ingredients

- 1 cup green lentils
- 1 cup brown lentils
- 1 bay leaf
- 2 garlic cloves minced
- 2 Roma tomatoes seeded and diced
- 1 green pepper seeded and diced
- ½ cup pitted kalamata olives
- 2 cucumbers peeled seeded and diced
- 1 cup crumbled feta cheese for garnish

Ingredients - Vinaigrette

- 1 tablespoon Dijon mustard
- 2 tablespoons white wine vinegar
- ½ cup virgin olive oil
- 1 tablespoon dry oregano
- Salt and pepper to taste

Whisk the dressing together until combined evenly.

Putting It All Together

- Add the lentils, garlic and bay leaf to a pot and fill with cold water 2 inches from the top
- Cover and boil for 15 minutes then drain under cold water
- Combine garlic, Roma tomatoes, green pepper, kalamata olives, and cucumbers
- Combine all ingredients and lightly drizzle the salad with the vinaigrette and top with feta cheese

Serves 4 people

Kimchi Noodle Salad on Rice Cake Bowl

Ingredients

- 1 cup chopped kimchi
- 2 minced garlic cloves
- 1 teaspoon fresh ginger grated
- 1 teaspoon sesame oil
- 2 tablespoons sugar
- 2 tablespoons rice wine vinegar
- 1 teaspoon Gochutgaru paste
- 2 packets Soba noodles cooked according to package
- 1 carrot peeled and cut into julienne
- ½ red onion sliced julienne
- 8-inch spring roll wrappers
- Vegetable oil for frying
- Black and white sesame seeds for garnish
- ½ cup scallions cut diagonally for garnish

Putting It All Together

- Combine kimchi, garlic cloves, ginger, sesame oil, sugar, rice wine vinegar, Gochutgaru paste, soba noodles, carrots and red onion
- Heat a large skillet with ½ inch vegetable oil on medium heat
- Once oil is hot put 1 spring roll wrapper at a time in the oil and hold down with metal tongs for about 5 to 8 seconds or until the wrapper puffs up into a bowl
- Remove the bowl and lay upside down onto a paper towel to drain excess oil
- Continue to fry the other wrappers until you have enough bowls for service
- Fill each bowl with the kimchi mixture and top with sesame seeds and scallions

Note: You can make the bowls up to 8 hours ahead of time.

Serves 4 people

Mango, Avocado and Goat Cheese Salad

Ingredients

- 1 small bag of mixed field greens
- 2 ripe mangos peeled, pitted and sliced
- 2 ripe avocados peeled, pitted and sliced
- ½ red onion sliced
- ½ cup goat cheese crumbled
- ¼ cup toasted slivered almonds
- Salt and pepper to taste
- Bread sticks

Ingredients - Mango Vinaigrette Dressing

- 1 ripe mango peeled and pitted
- ½ cup water
- ¼ cup olive oil
- 3 tablespoons honey
- 3 tablespoons apple cider vinegar
- Pinch of red pepper flakes
- Salt and pepper to taste

Add all the ingredients to a blender and puree until smooth

Putting It All Together

- Place the mango on top of a bed of greens, avocado, and red onion
- Lightly drizzle the vinaigrette dressing over the salad and top with goat cheese and toasted almonds
- Serve with bread sticks

Serves 4 people

Poached Pear Stuffed Gorgonzola

Ingredients

- 4 Bartlett or Bosc pears
- 2 cups dry red wine
- 1 cup orange juice
- ½ cup sugar
- 1 cinnamon stick
- 1 Star anise
- ½ cup Gorgonzola
- 1 small bag of arugula greens

Ingredients - Champagne Vinaigrette Dressing

- 1 tablespoon minced shallot
- 4 tablespoons champagne vinegar
- ½ teaspoon Dijon mustard
- ½ cup virgin olive oil
- Salt and pepper to taste

Whisk all the ingredients until blended well.

Putting It All Together

- Peel the pears leaving the stem intact for presentation and place into a deep saucepan
- Pour wine, orange juice and sugar over pears with the cinnamon stick and anise, poach until tender on medium heat
- Remove the pears from the poaching liquid and let cool
- Hollow the middle of pear and stuff each one with the Gorgonzola
- Place on bed of arugula greens and lightly drizzle with the champagne dressing

Serves 4 people

Pomegranate and Persimmon Salad with Lemon Lavender Vinaigrette

Ingredients

- 1 bag of mixed field greens
- 1 (4 ounce) goat cheese
- 2 Persimmons peeled and cut into wedges
- 2 Pomegranates seeded
- ½ cup toasted sliver almond

Ingredients - Lemon Lavender Vinaigrette

- ½ cup virgin olive oil
- 4 tablespoons lemon juice
- 2 garlic cloves minced
- 1 tablespoon honey
- 1 teaspoon dry lavender buds
- Salt and pepper to taste

Shake everything together in a jar and refrigerate until service.

Putting It All Together

- In a bowl assemble greens, persimmons, pomegranate and almonds
- Toss gently and lightly drizzle the vinaigrette to coat
- Top with crumbled goat cheese

Serves 4 people

Red and Yellow Roasted Beet Salad with Pistachios

Ingredients

- 1 bag of mixed green lettuce
- 3 red beets
- 3 yellow beets
- ½ red onion cut into matchsticks
- ½ cup shelled pistachios
- ½ cup crumbled goat cheese
- Bread twist or toasted dark rye bread

Ingredients - Apple Cider Vinaigrette Dressing

- ¼ cup apple cider vinegar
- 2 tablespoons rice vinegar
- ½ cup olive oil
- 2 teaspoons honey
- 1 teaspoon Dijon mustard
- Salt and pepper to taste

Shake everything together in a jar and refrigerate until service.

Putting It All Together

- Preheat oven to 400 degrees
- Wrap each medium size beet in foil and bake for 1 hour
- Unwrap beets and prick with a knife to make sure they are cooked all the way through
- Peel the skin and cut the beets into matchsticks, toss with the red onion
- Place the salad on a bed of greens
- Lightly drizzle dressing over salad, top with goat cheese and pistachios
- Serve with bread twist or toasted dark rye bread

Serves 4 people

Watercress, Radish, and Onion Salad with Poppyseed Honey Vinaigrette

Ingredients

- 1 bunch of watercress washed and drained
- 1 bunch of radishes sliced into matchsticks
- ½ red onion sliced
- 1 carrot peeled and sliced into matchsticks
- Toasted French bread

Ingredients - Poppyseed Honey Vinaigrette

- 1/3 cup Canola oil
- ¼ cup honey
- 2 tablespoons cider vinegar
- 2 teaspoons poppyseed
- ½ teaspoon salt

Shake everything together in a jar and refrigerate until service.

Putting It All Together

- Combine the salad ingredients in a bowl and toss
- Lightly drizzle the salad with dressing
- Serve on a plate with toasted French bread

Serves 4 people

Granitas . . .

- ❖ Apple Cinnamon Pie Granita
- ❖ Blueberry Lemon Granita
- ❖ Cantaloupe Granita
- ❖ Coconut Cherry Granita
- ❖ Cucumber Lime Granita
- ❖ Fiery Tomato Basil Granita
- ❖ Honey Dew Mint Granita
- ❖ Japanese Egg Plant and Basil Granita
- ❖ Mandarin Orange Granita
- ❖ Mango Lime Granita
- ❖ Peach Mint Coconut Granita
- ❖ Peach Sangria Granita
- ❖ Pineapple Cranberry Granita
- ❖ Pink Grapefruit Granita
- ❖ Plum Granita
- ❖ Prickly Pear Granita
- ❖ Roasted Red Beet Granita
- ❖ Sweet Chili Lychee Ginger Granita
- ❖ Watermelon Granita

Apple Cinnamon Pie Granita

Ingredients

- 2 (15 ounce) cans of apple pie filling
- 3 cups apple juice
- ½ cup sugar
- 2 tablespoons lemon juice
- ½ teaspoon cinnamon
- ¼ teaspoon ground nutmeg
- Dehydrated apple slices for garnish

Putting It All Together

- In a saucepan combine all the ingredients together and cook for 5 minutes, stirring until everything is well incorporated
- Put mixture into a deep-dish container with a cover and put in freezer for 3 to 4 hours
- Remove granita out of the freezer and with a fork scrape down until it resembles a snow cone like texture
- Put granita back in freezer until service time

Just before service time, take granita out 10 minutes ahead to thaw, scoop the granita into bowls, garnish with dehydrated apple slices.

Serves 6 people

Blueberry Lemon Granita

Ingredients

- 2 cups fresh blueberries
- ¼ cup lemon juice
- 1 cup water
- 1 cup coconut sugar
- 1 cinnamon stick
- 2 cloves
- Mint leaf for garnish

Putting It All Together

- In a heated saucepan, combine water and sugar until it dissolves
- Add blueberries, cinnamon, cloves and lemon juice, cook over low heat for 10 minutes
- Remove cinnamon stick and cloves, puree the mixture in a blender until smooth
- Put the mixture into a deep-dish container and freeze for 3 to 4 hours
- Remove granita out of the freezer and with a fork scrape down until it resembles a snow cone like texture
- Put granita back in freezer until service time

Just before service time, take granita out 10 minutes ahead to thaw, scoop the granita into bowls, garnish with mint leaf.

Serves 6 people

Cantaloupe Granita

Ingredients

- 1 cup water
- 1 cup sugar
- 2 cups cantaloupe peeled, seeded and cubed
- 2 tablespoons fresh lemon juice
- 1 teaspoon lemon zest
- Mint leaf for garnish

Putting It All Together

- In a small saucepan bring the water and sugar to a low boil until sugar has dissolved
- Let the liquid cool and combine with diced cantaloupe, lemon juice and zest, blend until smooth
- Put mixture into a deep-dish container with a cover and put in freezer for 3 to 4 hours
- Remove granita out of the freezer and with a fork scrape down until it resembles a snow cone like texture
- Put granita back in freezer until service time

Just before service time, take granita out 10 minutes ahead to thaw, scoop the granita into bowls, garnish with mint leaf.

Serves 6 people

Coconut Cherry Granita

Ingredients

- 2 (15 ounce) cans pitted cherries/ reserve liquid
- 1 cup reserve cherry juice
- 1 cup water
- 2 tablespoons lime juices
- ¼ cup cherry liqueur
- 1 cup coconut milk

Putting It All Together

- In a deep saucepan bring the reserve cherry juice, water, sugar and lime juice to a low boil until the sugar has dissolved,
- Blend the cherries, coconut milk and the liquid mixture until smooth
- Put mixture into a deep-dish container with a cover and put in freezer for 3 to 4 hours
- Remove granita out of the freezer and with a fork scrape down until it resembles a snow cone like texture
- Put granita back in freezer until service time

Just before service time, take granita out 10 minutes ahead to thaw, scoop the granita into bowls.

Serves 6 people

Cucumber Lime Granita

Ingredients

- 2 cucumbers peeled, seeded and diced
- 3 tablespoons fresh mint chopped fine
- ½ cup water
- ½ cup sugar
- 3 tablespoons fresh squeezed lime juice
- Mint sprig for garnish

Putting It All Together

- In a saucepan heat the water and sugar to a low boil until the sugar has dissolved
- Re move from heat and let cool
- In a blender combine the diced cucumber, lime juice and mint and liquid, blend until smooth
- Put mixture into a deep-dish container with a cover and put in freezer for 3 to 4 hours
- Remove granita out of the freezer and with a fork scrape down until it resembles a snow cone like texture
- Put granita back in freezer until service time

Just before service time, take granita out 10 minutes ahead to thaw, scoop the granita into bowls, garnish with a sprig of mint.

Serves 4 people

Fiery Tomato Basil Granita

Ingredients

- 4 pounds of ripe tomatoes peeled and seeded
- ½ cup fresh basil, stems removed
- 1 garlic clove finely minced
- ¼ teaspoon red pepper flakes
- 1 tablespoon red wine vinegar
- 2 teaspoons olive oil
- Salt and pepper to taste

Putting It All Together

- In a blender puree all the ingredients together until smooth
- Put mixture into a deep-dish container with a cover and put in freezer for 3 to 4 hours
- Remove granita out of the freezer and with a fork scrape down until it resembles a snow cone like texture
- Put granita back in freezer until service time

Just before service time, take granita out 10 minutes ahead to thaw, scoop the granita into bowls, garnish with a fresh basil leaf.

Serves 4 people

Honeydew Mint Granita

Ingredients

- 2 cups diced honeydew
- 1 cup water
- 1 cup coconut sugar
- 2 tablespoons fresh mint chopped
- 2 teaspoons lemon juice
- Mint leaf for garnish

Putting It All Together

- In a small saucepan heat the water and sugar until it dissolves on low boil
- Remove from heat and let cool
- Combine diced honeydew, mint, and lemon juice in a blender, puree until smooth
- Put mixture into a deep-dish container with a cover and put in freezer for 3 to 4 hours
- Remove granita out of the freezer and with a fork scrape down until it resembles a snow cone like texture
- Put granita back in freezer until service time

Just before service time, take granita out 10 minutes ahead to thaw, scoop the granita into bowls, garnish with a mint leaf.

Serves 6 people

Japanese Eggplant and Basil Granita

Ingredients

- 3 Japanese Eggplant peeled, seeded and diced
- 5 medium size basil leaf without stems
- 1 cup water
- 1 cup sugar
- 3 tablespoons lemon juice
- Pinch of salt
- Mint sprig for garnish

Putting It All Together

- In a saucepan bring the water and sugar to low boil until sugar has dissolved
- Add the eggplant, basil, lemon juice and salt, cook for 10 to 15 minutes and let cool
- Combine all ingredients in blender, puree the mixture until smooth
- Put mixture into a deep-dish container with a cover and put in freezer for 3 to 4 hours
- Remove granita out of the freezer and with a fork scrape down until it resembles a snow cone like texture
- Put granita back in freezer until service time

Just before service time, take granita out 10 minutes ahead to thaw, scoop the granita into bowls, garnish with a sprig of mint.

Serves 4 people

Mandarin Orange Granita

Ingredients

- 1 (15 ounce) can mandarin orange reserve liquid
- 1/3 cup sugar
- 1/3 cup reserved juice
- 3 tablespoons lemon juice

Putting It All Together

- In a saucepan add the sugar, reserved juice and lemon juice, cook until sugar has dissolved over a low boil
- Add the mandarin orange and cook for another 5 minutes
- Put mixture into a deep-dish container with a cover and put in freezer for 3 to 4 hours
- Remove from heat and let cool then puree in a blender
- Remove granita out of the freezer and with a fork scrape down until it resembles a snow cone like texture
- Put granita back in freezer until service time

Just before service time, take granita out 10 minutes ahead to thaw, scoop the granita into bowls.

Serves 4 people

Mango Lime Granita

Ingredients

- 1 (16 ounce) can diced mango reserve liquid
- ¼ cup lime juice
- ½ cup reserved mango juice
- ½ cup water
- 1 cup sugar

Putting It All Together

- In a saucepan combine water mango juice and sugar together and heat on low boil until sugar has dissolved
- Remove from heat and cool, add the diced mango, blend everything together until smooth
- Put mixture into a deep-dish container with a cover and put in freezer for 3 to 4 hours
- Remove granita out of the freezer and with a fork scrape down until it resembles a snow cone like texture
- Put granita back in freezer until service time

Just before service time, take granita out 10 minutes ahead to thaw, scoop the granita into bowls.

Serves 4 people

Peach Mint Coconut Granita

Ingredients

- 2 (15 ounce) can peaches diced and reserve juice
- 1 cup reserved peach juice
- 1 cup water
- 1 tablespoon lemon juice
- 1 tablespoon minced fresh mint
- 1 can coconut milk
- Mint sprig for garnish

Putting It All Together

- In a deep saucepan bring reserve peach juice, water, and sugar to a low boil until sugar has dissolved
- Remove from heat and let cool, add the chopped peaches, mint, lemon juice, and coconut and blend until mixture is smooth
- Put mixture into a deep-dish container with a cover and put in freezer for 3 to 4 hours
- Remove granita out of the freezer and with a fork scrape down until it resembles a snow cone like texture
- Put granita back in freezer until service time

Just before service time, take granita out 10 minutes ahead to thaw, scoop the granita into bowls, garnish with a sprig of mint.

Serves 6 people

Pina Colada Granita

Ingredients

- 2 (14 ounce) cans of pineapple chunks reserve liquid
- 1/3 cup sugar
- 1/3 cup pineapple juice
- 1/3 cup dark rum
- 1 cup coconut milk
- ¼ cup toasted coconut or toasted almonds for garnish

Putting It All Together

- Combine all the ingredients together in a blender and puree until smooth
- Put mixture into a deep-dish container with a cover and put in freezer for 3 to 4 hours
- Remove granita out of the freezer and with a fork scrape down until it resembles a snow cone like texture
- Put granita back in freezer until service time

Just before service time, take granita out 10 minutes ahead to thaw, scoop the granita into bowls, garnish with toasted coconut or toasted almonds for an in between dinner course or as a dessert.

Serves 4 people

Pineapple Cranberry Granita

Ingredients

- 2 (15 ounce) cans of pineapple chunks
- ½ package frozen cranberries
- 1/3 cup water
- 1/3 cup sugar
- 3 tablespoons lemon juice
- 1 cup coconut milk
- ¼ cup toasted coconut for garnish

Putting It All Together

- In a saucepan combine the first 5 ingredients and cook 10 to 15 minutes until the cranberries have broken up
- Add the coconut milk and let cool
- In a blender puree all the ingredients until smooth
- Put mixture into a deep-dish container with a cover and put in freezer for 3 to 4 hours
- Remove granita out of the freezer and with a fork scrape down until it resembles a snow cone like texture
- Put granita back in freezer until service time

Just before service time, take granita out 10 minutes ahead to thaw, scoop the granita into bowls, garnish with toasted coconut.

Serves 6 people

Pink Grapefruit Granita with a Splash of Champagne

Ingredients

- 2 (15 ounce) cans of pink grapefruit section / reserve juice
- 1 cup water
- 1 cup reserved grapefruit juice
- 1 cup sugar
- 1 teaspoon lime juice
- 1 teaspoon lime zest
- Splash of champagne for garnish

Putting It All Together

- Combine in a saucepan on medium heat grapefruit juice, water and sugar until sugar has dissolved
- Remove from heat and let cool
- In a blender combine cool liquid, grapefruit sections, lime juice and zest
- Puree until mixture is smooth
- Put mixture into a deep-dish container with a cover and put in freezer for 3 to 4 hours
- Remove granita out of the freezer and with a fork scrape down until it resembles a snow cone like texture
- Put granita back in freezer until service time

Just before service time, take granita out 10 minutes ahead to thaw, scoop the granita into bowls, top off with a splash of champagne.

Serves 6 people

Plum Granita

Ingredients

- 1 (14 ounce) can plums peeled and pitted
- ½ cup red wine
- 1/3 cup water
- 1/3 cup sugar
- 1 teaspoon grated ginger
- 2 tablespoons honey
- ½ cinnamon stick
- 1 tablespoon lemon juice

Putting it all Together

- Put all the ingredients together in a saucepan and cook for 20 minutes
- Remove cinnamon stick, remove from heat and let cool
- Puree the granita until smooth
- Put mixture into a deep-dish container with a cover and put in freezer for 3 to 4 hours
- Remove granita out of the freezer and with a fork scrape down until it resembles a snow cone like texture
- Put granita back in freezer until service time

Just before service time, take granita out 10 minutes ahead to thaw, scoop the granita into bowls.

Serves 4 people

Prickly Pear Granita

Ingredients

- 1 cup water
- 1 cup sugar
- 8 Prickly pear cactus fruit peeled
- ¼ cup lime juice
- 2 teaspoons lime zest

Putting It All Together

- In a saucepan combine water and sugar and bring to a low boil until sugar has dissolved
- Remove from heat and let cool
- Dice the cactus fruit and place into a blender with the sugar water, lime juice and puree until smooth
- Strain the mixture to extract the solids so you are left with only the juice
- Add lime zest and put the cactus liquid into a deep-dish container with a cover and put in freezer for 3 to 4 hours
- Remove granita out of the freezer and with a fork scrape down until it resembles a snow cone like texture
- Put granita back in freezer until service time

Just before service time, take granita out 10 minutes ahead to thaw, scoop the granita into bowls.

Serves 4 people

Roasted Red Beet Granita

Ingredients

- 4 medium size fresh beets
- 1 cup beet juice
- 1 cup sugar
- 1 teaspoon lemon juice
- 5 cups water
- Lemon wedge for garnish

Putting It All Together

- Preheat oven to 350 degrees
- Clean beets with a brush under warm water then rub with olive oil and sea salt
- Wrap each one in foil and bake for 1 hour or until fork tender
- Remove the beets and let cool until you can safely handle them
- Peel the kin off and cube into bite sized chunks (I recommend that you wear food safe gloves to avoid staining)
- Add 5 cups of water and beet juice into a saucepan on low heat and cook until sugar has dissolved
- Add the beets and lemon juice, cook for another 10 minutes
- Remove from heat and let cool then place the beet granita in a blender and puree until smooth
- Put mixture into a deep-dish container with a cover and put in freezer for 3 to 4 hours
- Remove granita out of the freezer and with a fork scrape down until it resembles a snow cone like texture
- Put granita back in freezer until service time

Just before service time, take granita out 10 minutes ahead to thaw, scoop the granita into bowls, garnish with lemon wedge.

Serves 4 people

Sweet Chili Lychee Ginger Granita

Ingredients

- 1 (15 ounce) can lychee w/reserved juice
- ½ cup water
- ½ cup lychee juice
- 1 cup sugar
- ½ cup sweet chili sauce
- 1 teaspoon lime juice
- 1 teaspoon fresh grated ginger
- 1 teaspoon lime zest

Putting It All Together

- In a small saucepan over medium heat combine water, lychee juice and sugar
- Cook until sugar is dissolved, remove from heat and let cool
- In a blender combine Lychee, sweet chili sauce, lime juice, 1 teaspoon lime zest, ginger and liquid syrup blend until smooth
- Put mixture into a deep-dish container with a cover and put in freezer for 3 to 4 hours
- Remove granita out of the freezer and with a fork scrape down until it resembles a snow cone like texture
- Put granita back in freezer until service time

Just before service time, take granita out 10 minutes ahead to thaw, scoop the granita into bowls.

Serves 4 people

Watermelon Granita

Ingredients

- ½ pound seedless melon
- ¼ cup sugar
- ¼ cup lime juice
- 1 tablespoon lime zest
- Mint leaf for garnish

Putting It All Together

- Remove the watermelon rind and cube the watermelon
- Add the cubed melon, sugar, lime, and zest in a blender
- Puree the ingredients together until smooth
- Put mixture into a deep-dish container with a cover and put in freezer for 3 to 4 hours
- Remove granita out of the freezer and with a fork scrape down until it resembles a snow cone like texture
- Put granita back in freezer until service time

Just before service time, take granita out 10 minutes ahead to thaw, scoop the granita into bowls, garnish with mint leaf.

Serves 4 people

Entrées . . .

- ❖ Almond Crusted Pork Tenderloin with Jalapeno Plum Sauce
- ❖ Chicken Bismark with Jasmine Rice
- ❖ Chorizo Stuffed with Black Bean Sauce
- ❖ Chicken Scallopini with Artichoke Lemon Caper Sauce
- ❖ Chicken Stuffed with Herb Pimento Cream Cheese
- ❖ Chicken Stuffed with Capicola, Blue Cheese with Mushroom Sauce
- ❖ Chicken Stuffed with Artichoke with Bechamel Sauce
- ❖ Corned Beef and Cabbage with Fall Vegetables
- ❖ Cornmeal Crusted Catfish with Jalapeno Cilantro Sauce
- ❖ Cornmeal Crusted Tilapia with Puttanesca Sauce
- ❖ English Braised Short Ribs
- ❖ Italian Short Ribs with Parmesan Polenta
- ❖ Jamaican Chicken with Papaya and Mango Salsa
- ❖ Lamb Satay with Peanut Sauce
- ❖ Lobster Thermidor
- ❖ Mandarin Orange Dijon Chicken
- ❖ Osso Buco with Gremolata
- ❖ Pistachio Crusted Pork Tenderloin with Jalapeno Plum Sauce
- ❖ Pork Tenderloin Grilled with Mediterranean Salsa
- ❖ Salmon en Papillote
- ❖ Salmon Wrapped Puff Pastry with Saffron Orange Sauce
- ❖ Stuffed Peppercorn Crusted Pork Tenderloin
- ❖ Stuffed Quail in Butternut Squash Sauce
- ❖ Stuffed Turkey Roulade with Sage Mushroom Sauce
- ❖ Thai Salmon with Bangkok Curry Sauce
- ❖ Wrapped Salmon in Phyllo with Mornay Sauce

Almond Crusted Pork Tenderloin with Jalapeno Plum Sauce

Ingredients

- 2 pounds pork tenderloin
  - Trim away fat and silver skin off tenderloin
- Salt and Pepper to taste
- 1 tablespoon Dijon mustard
- 4 ounces blanched almonds finely chopped
- ½ cup dry breadcrumbs finely chopped
- 1 garlic clove minced
- 1 tablespoon fresh chopped thyme

Ingredients - Jalapeno Plum Sauce

- 1 ½ tablespoon vegetable oil
- 1 tablespoon lemon juice
- ¼ cup chopped red onion
- ½ cup honey
- 1 tablespoon minced garlic
- 3 tablespoons soy sauce
- 2 tablespoons seeded and chopped jalapeno
- 1 ½ teaspoons allspice
- 2 (15 ounce) cans of purple plums pitted and diced
- 1 ½ teaspoons curry

Sauté the onions, garlic and jalapeno in oil until tender. Add the remaining ingredients and cook uncovered for 30 minutes.

Putting It All Together

- Preheat oven to 400 degrees
- Season the tenderloin with salt and pepper then rub with mustard
- Combine the 4 ounces blanched almonds finely chopped, ½ cup dry breadcrumbs finely chopped, 1 garlic clove minced, 1 tablespoon fresh chopped thyme and roll the mixture onto the tenderloin
- Roast the tenderloin on a wire rack in the oven for 30 minutes until the internal temperature reaches 145 degrees
- Remove the tenderloin from the oven and let it rest until service time
- Serve with the Jalapeno Plum Sauce.

Serves 4-6 people

Chicken Bismark with Jasmine Rice

Ingredients

- 4 (6ounce) pieces of chicken
- ½ each green and red pepper diced
- ½ cup red onion diced
- ½ cup carrot diced and lightly poached in water
    - Cook onion, carrot, green and red pepper till fork tender in water
- 1 cup white mushrooms quartered
- 1 tablespoon of fresh chopped thyme
- ¼ cup olive oil
- 4 tablespoons butter
- ½ cup dry white wine or sherry
- ½ cup all-purpose flour
- 2 cups chicken stock
- Serve with Jasmine rice

Cook green and red peppers with carrots until fork tender in water.

Putting It All Together

- Pan sauté the chicken breast in hot olive oil and butter on both sides for 3 minutes each
- Remove from skillet, let cool and dice into cubes
- In the same skillet deglaze the pan with white wine or sherry to scrape the fond that is left on the bottom of pan
- Add the flour to make a roux, once mixed together add the chicken stock to make a creamy like texture
- Combine the chicken and vegetables in the cream sauce then add heavy cream to finish

Salt and pepper to taste, best served with Jasmine rice.

Serves 4 people

Chicken Scallopini with Artichoke Lemon Caper Sauce

Ingredients

- 4 (6 ounce) chicken breast
- Kosher salt and pepper
- Flour for dredging
- 6 tablespoons butter
- 4 tablespoons olive oil
- ¼ cup dry white wine
- 1/3 cup lemon juice
- ¼ cup chicken stock
- ¼ cup capers
- 4 tablespoons chop parsley
- 1 cup can chopped artichoke
- Chopped parsley for garnish

Putting It All Together

- Dredge the chicken in flour with salt and pepper
- Sauté chicken in a hot pan with butter and olive oil on both sides for 1 minute each until golden brown
- Remove chicken from skillet and set aside on a plate
- In the same skillet deglaze the pan with white wine and reduce by half
- Add lemon juice, chicken stock, capers and artichoke
- Place the chicken back into the skillet and cook for a few minutes longer

Sprinkle with chop parsley and serve.

Serves 4 people

Chicken Stuffed Artichoke with Bechamel Sauce

Ingredients

- 4 (6 ounce) Boneless Chicken Breast
- 1 (14 ounce) can Artichoke hearts drain and chopped
- 1 carrot peeled and diced
- 1 celery rib diced
- ¼ cup diced yellow onion
- 2 garlic cloves minced
- ¼ cup finely chopped fresh spinach
- 1 tablespoon dry oregano
- 1 (8 ounce) cream cheese room temperature
- ¼ cup parmesan cheese
- Serve with pasta and asparagus

Ingredients - Basil Béchamel Sauce

- 2 tablespoons butter melted
- 1 cup milk
- 2 tablespoons flour
- ½ cup fresh chopped basil

In a saucepan melt butter and add flour to make a roux. Add milk and stir until it becomes smooth. Add pinch of nutmeg, chopped basil, salt and pepper. Serve warm.

Putting It All Together

- Preheat oven to 350 degrees
- Cut a pocket in each chicken breast, set aside
- Sauté onion, garlic, carrot and celery in a little bit of olive oil until tender and set aside to cool
- Combine in a bowl chopped artichoke, the cool vegetables, spinach, cream cheese and oregano; mix well
- Divide the mixture into four portions and stuff into the chicken
- Lightly bread the stuff chicken breast with flour, egg wash and the panko breadcrumbs
- Secure with toothpicks, place onto baking sheet and bake at for 20 to 25 minutes

Serve with Béchamel Sauce, pasta and fresh asparagus.

Serves 4 people

Chicken Stuffed with Capicola and Gruyere with Creamy Mushroom Sauce

Ingredients

- 4 (6 ounce) boneless chicken breasts
- 8 slices Capicola
- 8 slices Gruyere cheese
- ¼ cup flour seasoned with salt and pepper
- 1 egg mixed with 1 tablespoon water
- Breadcrumbs mixed with 1 tablespoon oregano
- 3 tablespoons vegetable oil
- Parsley or chive for garnish
- Serve with pasta, rice, or whip potato of your choice and fresh vegetables

Ingredients - Creamy Mushroom Sauce

- 2 tablespoons butter
- 1 tablespoon finely chopped shallot
- 1 clove of garlic minced
- ½ pound mushrooms sliced thin
- 2 tablespoons flour
- 1 tablespoon Marsala wine or brandy
- ½ cup chicken stock
- 1/2 cup heavy cream or half and half
- Salt and pepper to taste

Creamy Mushroom Sauce - Putting It All Together

- In a hot skillet sauté shallot, garlic and mushrooms together until golden brown
- Deglaze the pan with Marsala wine or brandy
- Cook for 1 minute, add flour to make a roux
- Slowly whisk the chicken stock until it has thickened, cook for another minute
- To finish, add heavy cream or half and half, season with salt and pepper to taste

Add chopped parsley or chives for garnish. I suggest you serve the dish with pasta, rice, or whip potato of your choice and fresh vegetables.

Putting It All Together

- Pound the chicken evenly with a mallet, slit a pocket halfway into the chicken
- Place one piece each of the capicola and gruyere in the pocket and flour both sides of chicken
- Dredge into the egg wash and then coat with breadcrumbs
- Sauté the chicken in a hot skillet with the oil on both sides until lightly gold brown

Set aside on a plate while you prepare the mushroom sauce.

Serves 4 people

Corned Beef & Cabbage with Fall Vegetables

Ingredients

- 4 pounds corned beef
- 1 large yellow onion
- Bouquet garni: 2 sprigs of Parsley, 2 sprigs of fresh Thyme, 1 Bay Leaf (tie the herbs in a small cheese cloth with string)
- 5 medium size carrots peeled and trimmed and cut into small bite size pieces
- 1 small head of cabbage cut into 6 to 8 wedges
- 3 small turnips peeled and trimmed – cut into one-inch pieces
- 10 small red potatoes washed in cold water – cut into one-inch pieces

Putting It All Together

- Rinse the corned beef in cold water and place it in a large stock pot add water to the top of corned beef
- Then add bouquet garni, onion, and bring to a boil, turn heat down and spoon out any froth that has floated to the top
- Cover with an airtight lid and cook for about 2 hours or until corned beef is fork tender
- Remove the corned beef out of stock pot and keep warm off to the side
- In the meantime, place cabbage, carrots, turnips and red potatoes in the stock pot and cook for about 20 minutes or until all vegetables are fork tender
- Remove the vegetables from the stock pot and place into serving bowl and discard the bouquet garni
- Slice the corned beef onto a serving platter garnish with parsley and serve with a side of Horse Radish sauce and Dijon mustard

Serves 6 people

Chorizo Stuffed Chicken with Black Bean Sauce

Ingredients

- 4 (6 ounce) chicken breasts
- 2 tablespoons olive oil
- 8 ounces of chorizo with casings removed
- ¼ cup onion chopped
- 2 garlic cloves minced
- 1 jalapeno seeded and finely diced
- 1 cup shredded pepper jack cheese
- Serve with Spanish rice and fresh vegetables

Ingredients - Black Bean Sauce

- 1 (15 ounce) can black beans
- ½ cup chicken stock
- ¼ cup chopped onions
- ¼ teaspoon cumin
- 1 garlic clove minced
- 2 tablespoons chopped cilantro
- Sour cream

Sauté onions and garlic until tender add black beans, cumin, chicken stock and cook for 10 minutes. Puree everything in blender except cilantro and sour cream until smooth. When ready to serve heat the black bean sauce and serve a dollop of sour cream and some chopped cilantro. Great with Spanish rice and fresh vegetables.

Putting It All Together

- Preheat oven to 350 degrees
- In a pan, sauté onion until translucent then add garlic and cook a few minutes longer
- Add chorizo and jalapeno, cook another 5 minutes, remove filling from pan and let cool
- Butterfly the chicken breast carefully slicing each breast horizontally stopping about ¼ inch from each end
- Combine the mixture with the cheese and stuff into the chicken
- Bake in oven for 30 minutes

Remove from oven and serve hot with black bean sauce.

Serves 4 people

Cornmeal Frito Crusted Catfish with Jalapeno Cilantro Cream Sauce

Ingredients

- 1 egg slightly beaten with 1 tablespoon water
- 2 tablespoons lemon juice
- ½ cup flour with ½ teaspoon Cajun spice
- ¼ cup yellow cornmeal and ¼ cup Frito's crushed together fine
- 4 fresh catfish deboned
- Chopped chive for garnish

Ingredients - Jalapeno Cilantro Cream Sauce

- 3 jalapenos seeded
- ½ cup fresh cilantro leaves
- 3 garlic cloves minced
- 1 tablespoon lime juice
- ½ cup mayonnaise
- ¼ cup heavy cream

Blend everything together until smooth, take the sauce out of blender and combine with the heavy cream. Adjust the seasoning with salt and pepper.

Putting It All Together

- Dredge the catfish in flour, then in egg wash and bread with the cornmeal and
- Frito's crust
- Pan fry the catfish on both sides until golden brown for about 1 to 2 minutes per side
- Garnish with the chop chives and side of room temperature Jalapeno Cilantro Cream Sauce and serve

Serves 4 people

Cornmeal Crusted Tilapia with Puttanesca Sauce

Ingredients

- 4 Fresh deboned Tilapia
- ½ cup flour seasoned lightly with salt and pepper
- ½ cup cornmeal mixed with 1 tablespoon dry oregano
- 1 egg slightly beaten with 1 tablespoon of water
- Vegetable oil
- Chopped parsley for garnish

Ingredients - Puttanesca Sauce

- ¼ cup olive oil
- 1 tablespoon tomato paste
- ½ cup chopped onion
- 2 tablespoons capers drained
- 4 cloves garlic minced
- 1 tablespoon minced anchovy
- 1 (28 ounce) can diced tomatoes
- ¼ teaspoon red pepper flakes
- ½ cup pitted sliced kalamata olives
- salt and pepper to taste

Sauté the onions in olive oil until slightly caramelized, then add garlic for 2 minutes. Add tomatoes and the rest of the ingredients, simmer until sauce has thickened and slightly reduced.

Putting It All Together

- Dredge catfish in flour then egg wash, bread with cornmeal crust
- Pan sauté in olive oil for 1 minute on both side until golden brown, set aside

Serve with Puttanesca Sauce over the Tilapia, garnish with chopped parsley.

Serves 4 people

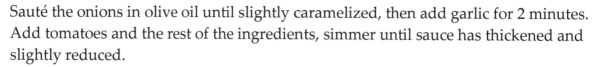

English Braised Short Ribs

Ingredients

- 4 pounds English style short ribs
- 4 tablespoons olive oil
- 1 cup diced yellow onion
- 4 garlic cloves minced
- ½ cup dry red wine
- 2 cups beef stock
- 2 tablespoons tomato paste
- 1 teaspoon dry thyme
- 1 cup mushrooms sliced
- Chopped parsley for garnish
- Serve with your choice of butter noodles, polenta, rice or mashed potatoes and a fresh vegetable of your choice

Putting It All Together

- Preheat oven to 350 degrees
- Remove ribs from the refrigerator and let rest at room temperature for 30 minutes
- In a hot Dutch oven add oil and sear the ribs on all sides until brown
- Add additional oil if the meat starts to stick or burn
- Remove ribs and set aside
- Add onions and garlic to the Dutch oven, sauté for a few minutes
- Add the red wine and reduce by half, then add beef stock, tomato paste and thyme; stir and bring to a boil
- Return the ribs back to the Dutch oven, cover and place in the oven for 2 1/2 hours or until fork tender
- Add the mushrooms and cook for 30 minutes longer
- Remove the ribs and place on a platter, cover to let rest
- Reduce sauce until it thickens, then skim the fat

Serve the ribs on individual plates with sauce laced on top, sprinkle with chop parsley. English short ribs are best served with your choice of butter noodles, polenta, rice or mashed potatoes and a fresh vegetable of your choice.

Serves 4 people

Grilled Pork Tenderloin with Mediterranean Salsa

Ingredients

- 1-pound pork tenderloin - Trim away fat and silver skin off tenderloin
- Serving with Basmati rice or couscous

Ingredients - Dry Rub for Tenderloin

- 1 tablespoon olive oil
- 2 garlic cloves minced fine
- 1 teaspoon oregano
- ½ teaspoon thyme
- 1 teaspoon smoke paprika
- ½ teaspoon onion powder
- Salt and pepper to taste

Ingredients - Mediterranean Salsa

- 1 cup grape tomatoes cut in half
- ½ cup diced red onion
- ¼ cup pitted kalamata olives
- ½ cup peeled and diced cucumber
- 3 tablespoons capers drained well
- 2 tablespoons chopped basil
- 1 garlic clove minced fine
- 1 to 2 tablespoons olive oil
- 2 teaspoons lemon juice
- ½ teaspoon grated lemon zest
- 1 tablespoon chopped parsley
- Salt and pepper to taste

Putting It All Together

- In a bowl combine all the ingredients together and mix well. Put the salsa to rest in the refrigerator for about 20 minutes allowing the ingredients to infuse before service time.

Putting It All Together

- Preheat a cast iron grill over medium heat
- Clean the tenderloin of any silver skin and fat
- Mix oil and the rest of the ingredients together in a small bowl
- Rub the mixture all over the tenderloin
- Spray the skillet with cooking spray lightly and grill the tenderloin on all sides for about 2 minutes per side
- Remove the tenderloin from the skillet and let rest 5 minutes

Slice the tenderloin as desired, serve with Mediterranean Salsa. Recommend serving with Basmati rice or couscous.

Serves 4 people

Italian Short Ribs with Parmesan Polenta

Ingredients

- 6 pounds lean short ribs
- ¼ cup seasoned four with salt and pepper
- 3 tablespoons olive oil
- 1 medium diced onion
- 3 garlic cloves minced
- 2 teaspoons dry Italian seasoning
- ½ teaspoon dry red pepper flakes
- 2 carrots peeled and diced
- 2 celery ribs diced
- 1 cup dry red wine
- 2 tablespoons tomato paste
- 1 (28 ounce) can diced tomatoes
- 1 ½ cups beef stock
- ¼ cup chopped parsley for garnish

Ingredients - Creamy Parmesan Polenta

- 4 cups water
- 1 cup milk
- 1 teaspoon salt
- 1 cup yellow corn meal
- 4 tablespoons butter
- ½ cup grated parmesan cheese

In a saucepan bring water and milk to a boil add salt, gradually pour the polenta into the pan whisking slowly. Turn down the heat and cover for 25 minutes, stir occasionally so it doesn't stick to the bottom of pan. When done add a bit more milk if needed to make it creamer and then add Parmesan cheese to finish.

Putting It All Together

- Dredge the short ribs in the flour mixture and then brown the ribs in a hot skillet with olive oil on all sides until brown on all sides – just about one minute
- Transfer to a plate then add onions, garlic, carrots, celery, and seasoning to the pan and sauté for 5 minutes
- Add tomato paste and the red wine and cook until wine has reduced by half
- Add the diced tomatoes and beef stock, bring to a boil then transfer the ribs back into the pot
- Reduce heat, cover and cook for 2 to 3 hours until fork tender
- Serve individually by placing polenta in a round shallow bowl and top with Italian short ribs and garnish with chopped parsley

Serves 4-6 people

Jamaican Chicken with Papaya and Mango Salsa

Ingredients

- 4 (6 ounce) chicken breasts
- 3 tablespoons Jerk seasoning
- 2 tablespoons olive oil
- 1 tablespoon apple cider vinegar
- Serve with a rice pilaf

Ingredients - Papaya Mango Salsa

- 1 Papaya peeled and diced
- 1 Mango peeled and diced
- ½ red onion diced
- 1 small jalapeno seeded and diced
- ½ each red and green bell pepper diced
- 2 tablespoons lime juice
- Salt and pepper to taste

To make the salsa combine all the ingredients in a bowl refrigerate and serve until ready.

Putting It All Together

- Combine chicken, seasoning, olive oil, and vinegar in a zip lock bag and marinate for 1 hour
- Remove the chicken and discard the marinade
- Pan sauté the Jerk chicken 3 minutes on each side

Serve with rice pilaf and top with salsa.

Serves 4 people

Lobster Thermidor

Ingredients

- 4 (6 ounce) lobster tails
- ½ teaspoon old bay seasoning
- ½ teaspoon paprika
- 4 tablespoons butter
- 2 tablespoons parmesan cheese
- 1 small yellow onion finely diced
- 2 tablespoons panko breadcrumbs
- 2 tablespoons flour
- ¼ cup white wine or dry sherry
- ½ cup cream
- 1/3 cup grated white cheddar cheese
- Lemon wedges for garnish
- ¼ cup chopped parsley for garnish

Putting It All Together

- Bring a pot of water to boil
- Add lobster to boiling water for 5 minutes until lobster shell is fully red
- Drain lobster and shock under cold water to cool
- With a sharp scissors cut the underside of tail and remove the meat
- Reserve the shells and arrange in a shallow dish
- Take the meat and chop into small bite size pieces
- In a small pot add half the butter and sauté the onion until translucent
- To the same small pot melt the remaining butter and add chopped lobster meat
- Add flour and stir to mix then whisk in wine or sherry and the milk until even
- Add the cheese and old bay seasoning, salt and pepper to taste
- Pour the lobster mixture into the reserved tails
- Top the lobster mixture with a sprinkle of panko breadcrumbs, cheese and paprika
- Broil on high until the top of the lobster mixture is lightly brown, 2 to 3 minutes
- Remove the lobster from the oven

Top with chopped parsley, serve with wedge of lemon.

Serves 4 people

Mandarin Orange Dijon Chicken Thighs

Ingredients

- 8 to 10 chicken thighs
- 2 tablespoons Dijon mustard
- 3 tablespoons vegetable oil
- 1 cup mandarin orange jam
- ½ cup orange juice
- 1 teaspoon fresh grated ginger
- ¼ teaspoon red pepper flakes
- Salt and pepper to taste
- Small bag slivered almonds – toasted for garnish
- Chopped parsley for garnish
- Serve with Jasmine Rice and Broccolini

Putting It All Together

- Preheat skillet on medium
- Rub mustard on top of chicken thighs and sprinkle with salt and pepper
- Transfer chicken to the hot skillet and sauté in oil until golden brown, set aside on a plate
- Meanwhile in the same skillet combine jam, orange juice, grated ginger, and red pepper flakes
- Bring to boil then add the chicken thighs back into the skillet and turn the heat down, simmer for 30 minutes

Garnish with toasted slivered almonds and chop parsley, serve with Jasmine Rice and Broccolini.

Serves 4 people

Osso Buco with Gremolata

Ingredients

- 6 veal shanks (2 ½ pounds) cut by the butcher
- ¼ cup flour seasoned with paprika, salt and pepper
- 3 tablespoons butter
- 3 tablespoons olive oil
- 3 carrots peeled and diced
- 2 celery stalks diced
- 1 yellow onion chopped
- 2 garlic cloves minced
- 1 cup dry white wine
- ½ cup chicken stock
- ½ cup beef stock
- 28 ounce can of diced tomatoes
- 1 tablespoon tomato paste

Bouquet garni wrapped in cheese cloth

- 1 bay leaf
- 1 sprig Rosemary
- 1 sprig thyme

Combine 3 ingredients above and wrap in cheese cloth tied by an 8-inch string

Ingredients - Gremolata

- 1 bunch flat leaf parsley finely chopped
- 2 Garlic cloves finely minced
- Zest of 1 lemon
- 2 Teaspoons fresh lemon juice
- ½ cup olive oil
- ¼ teaspoon salt
- A pinch of red chili flakes

Putting It All Together

Combine all ingredients in a bowl and mix well, season if needed with salt and lemon. The Gremolata will be garnished on top of the Osso Buco.

Putting It All Together

- Season all sides of veal shank with the ¼ cup flour seasoned with paprika, salt and pepper

- Pan sear the shanks in a Dutch oven with olive oil and butter until golden brown on both sides
- Remove the shanks from the Dutch oven and set aside on a plate
- Add the diced carrots, celery, chopped yellow onion and 2 minced garlic cloves to the pan and cook for 5 minutes
- Deglaze the pan with white wine and place the shanks back into the Dutch oven along with the diced tomato, tomato paste, beef and chicken stock and bouquet garni tied with string to the handle of the Dutch oven
- Bring to a boil, reduce to low and simmer for 90 minutes
- Remove and discard the bouquet garni

Serve on individual plates topped with a teaspoon of Gremolata

Serves 4-6 people

Rainbow Trout with Jalapeno Sweet Corn Sauce

Ingredients

- 3 Trout split all in ½ and deboned by your fishmonger
- ¼ cup all-purpose flour
- ¼ tsp each salt and pepper
- 3 tablespoons butter
- Wedges of lemon for garnish

Ingredients - Creamy Jalapeno Sweet Corn Sauce

- 1 can (15 ounce) sweet corn
- 1 (8 ounce) cream cheese softened
- 2 jalapenos seeded and finely diced
- ¼ cup butter
- Salt and pepper to taste

Put all the ingredients together in a medium size pot cooking slowly over medium heat, stirring until well combined for about 10 minutes. Set aside and keep warm for serving over trout.

Putting It Together

- Dust each ½ of the trout with flour, lightly salt and pepper
- Pan fry the trout skin down in a hot skillet in butter for 3 to 4 minutes
- Flip the trout over and repeat

Serve the trout with a wedge of lemon and Sweet Corn Sauce.

Serves 4-6 people

Salmon en Papillote

Ingredients

- 4 (6 ounce) salmon deboned and skin removed
- ½ cup red onion sliced thin
- 1 zucchini julienned
- 1 large carrot julienned
- Olive oil
- ¼ cup fresh dill
- 2 whole lemons sliced thin
- Salt and pepper to taste
- Parchment paper for wrapping

Putting It All Together

- Preheat oven to 350 degrees
- In a bowl, mix vegetables together with olive oil, dill, salt and pepper
- Put each salmon on individual square parchment paper 8"X12"
- Top with vegetable mixture and about 4 slices of lemon
- Seal the parchment well by repeatedly folding the ends over each other taking care to make sure it is well sealed you don't want any steam to escape
- Lay each salmon in parchment on to a sheet pan and bake for 15 to 20 minutes, the salmon in the parchment will usually puff up

Place each individual packet on plate still sealed, then with a knife cut open the parchment at the table and enjoy.

Serves 4 people

Salmon Wrapped Puff Pastry with Saffron Orange Sauce

Ingredients - Salmon Puff Pastry

- 4 (8 ounce) salmon fillet
- 2 sheets frozen puff pastry
- 1 small orange cut in half
- 1 tablespoon lemon juice
- Lea and Perrins - dash
- ¼ cup dry white wine
- Chopped parsley for garnish
- Serve with rice and fresh asparagus

Ingredients - Saffron Orange Sauce

- 2 cups seafood stock
- 2 tablespoons butter
- 2 tablespoons flour
- ¼ teaspoon saffron
- ¼ cup orange juice
- ¼ cup heavy cream

Putting It All Together

Heat the fish stock, melt butter in saucepan and add flour, cook for 2 minutes. Add the fish stock and stir until it thickens. Add saffron, orange juice and sauté for another 5 minutes. Finish with heavy cream and whisk until smooth and velvet like. Set aside and keep warm for serving over salmon puff pastry.

Putting It All Together

- Preheat oven to 350 degrees
- Squeeze orange juice and lemon juice over salmon with a dash of Lea & Perrins over salmon lightly, marinate for 10 minutes
- Take puff pastry sheet and divide into 4 pieces to cover each salmon
- Sear all 4 fillets for 1 minute on both sides in a hot pan with a bit of oil
- Remove from heat and let cool, wrap each filet in the puff pastry and brush with egg wash (2 tablespoons water and egg whisked well)
- Bake for 10 to 15 minutes

Serve on individual plates by drizzling sauce over salmon and top with chopped parsley. Best served with rice and fresh asparagus.

Serves 4 people

Stuffed Chicken Breast with Honey Mustard Wasabi Black Bean Crust

Ingredients

- 4 (6 ounce) boneless chicken breasts
- 4 ounces cream cheese
- 1 (2 ounce) drained chop pimentos
- 1 garlic clove minced
- 1 teaspoon dry oregano
- 2 tablespoons chop parsley
- Serve with pasta, rice or potato of your choice, and fresh vegetables

Ingredients - Honey mustard wasabi black bean crust

- ¼ cup honey
- 1 tablespoon Dijon mustard
- ½ teaspoon powder wasabi
- 1 (15 ounce) can black beans
  - Rinse, drain and cook in oven for 30 minutes at 350 degrees
- 1 cup dry breadcrumbs

Putting It All Together

- Preheat oven to 350 degrees
- Flatten chicken breasts and with a mallet evenly
- Put a slit ¾ of the way from each end to make a pocket
- Mix the cream cheese, pimentos, garlic, oregano and parsley together in a bowl
- Stuff the cream cheese mixture into the chicken pocket
- Flour the chicken on both sides
- Sprinkle each breast lightly with salt and pepper
- Pan sauté the chicken on both sides in a hot skillet with vegetable oil until golden brown, cool and set aside
- In the meantime, take the black beans that have been dried from the oven and process in a blender with the breadcrumbs until coarsely chopped fine
- Brush each chicken breast with the honey wasabi mix and then place the black bean crust on each side of the chicken
- Place the chicken on to a sheet pan and bake in oven for 20 minutes.

Serve with pasta, rice or potato of your choice, and fresh vegetables.

Serves 4 people

Stuffed Peppercorn Crusted Pork Tenderloin

Ingredients

- 2 pounds pork tenderloin
- 1 tablespoon Dijon mustard
- 4 oz Boursin herb cream cheese
- ½ cup sundried tomato
- 1 cup can artichoke drained and chopped
- ¼ cup drained chopped pimentos
- 4 tablespoons mix peppercorn
- Serve with fresh vegetables and brown rice

Putting It All Together

- Remove silver skin and fat from tenderloin
- Butterfly the pork tenderloin in half
- Brush Dijon mustard lightly all over inside of the tenderloin
- Spread Boursin cheese evenly on tenderloin
- Top with artichoke and sundried tomato
- Roll tenderloin tightly and secure with butcher twine
- Brush tenderloin lightly all over with mustard and then peppercorn
- Heat frying pan and spray with cooking oil
- Brown tenderloin on all sides for 2 minutes each or until internal temperature is 145 degrees
- Remove tenderloin from pan and let rest for 5 minutes
- Remove the twine and slice tenderloin as desired

Serve on individual plates with mustard sauce, fresh vegetables and brown rice.

Serves 4-6 people

Stuffed Quail in Butternut Squash Sauce

Ingredients

- 4 (6 ounce) boneless quail
- 2 teaspoons chopped shallots
- 1 stick butter
- 1-pound mushrooms chopped fine
- 1 cup breadcrumbs
- 2 teaspoons fresh chopped sage
- 2 teaspoons chopped parsley
- 1 cup dry white wine
- Salt and pepper to taste

Ingredients - Butternut Squash Sauce

- 1 small butternut squash peeled, seeded and diced
- 2 tablespoons olive oil
- ¼ cup diced red onion
- Pinch of nutmeg
- 1 teaspoon chopped fresh sage
- 1 cup chicken stock
- ¼ cup heavy cream
- 2 tablespoons fresh chopped parsley
- 1 tablespoon of finely chopped shallots
- Salt and pepper to taste

Putting It All Together

- In a skillet on medium heat sauté shallots and red onions until lightly brown
- Add the cubed butternut squash, nutmeg, sage, and chicken stock, cook the squash for 10 minutes
- Transfer everything into a blender and puree until smooth
- Return the sauce to the skillet, add heavy cream and adjust the seasoning with salt and pepper and set aside for service time with quail

Putting It All Together

- Sauté shallots with 3 tablespoons butter then mix in the mushrooms, breadcrumbs, sage and parsley, deglaze with the wine and mix well
- Season the mixture with salt and pepper
- Stuff the mixture in the cavity of the quail.
- Melt the remaining butter in a sauté pan and brown the birds for 1 minute on each side,
- Turn the quail breast down, cover and cook in oven for 20 minutes
- Uncover and arrange breast side up, increase heat to 425 degrees and bake for 5 minutes or until the quail is nice and golden brown

Remove the quail from the oven and place the butternut squash sauce onto individual plates add the quail on top, garnish with chopped parsley - **Serves 4 people**

Stuffed Turkey Roulade with Sage Mushroom Sauce

Ingredients

- 2 to 3 pounds boneless turkey breast with skin
- 1-pound pork sausage
- ½ cup chopped onion
- 2 garlic cloves minced
- 2 celery ribs chopped fine
- 1 carrot peeled and diced fine
- ½ cup dry apricot diced
- 2 cups sourdough bread cubed
- 2 eggs
- ¼ cup milk
- 1 tablespoon fresh sage chop
- ½ teaspoon fresh chopped rosemary
- 1 tablespoon chop parsley
- Salt and pepper to taste

Ingredients - Sage Mushroom Sauce

- 3 tablespoons butter
- 1 tablespoon chopped shallot
- 1 clove garlic minced
- ½ pound variety mushrooms sliced thin
- 2 tablespoons fresh chopped sage
- 3 tablespoons flour
- ¼ cup dry white wine
- 1 cup chicken stock or turkey stock
- ½ cup heavy cream or half & half

In a hot skillet melt butter cook shallot, garlic and mushrooms until golden brown. Deglaze pan with white wine, add flour to make a roux and whisk the chicken stock slowly until it has thickened. Cook for another additional minute until sauce is smooth, add cream, sage, salt and pepper. Set aside for service time with turkey.

Putting It All Together

- Preheat oven to 375 degrees
- Cook sausage in a large sauté pan until fully cooked, remove with a slotted spoon leaving the grease in pan
- Add onion, garlic, celery, carrot and sauté for 5 minutes
- Remove from pan and combine the rest of the ingredients in a bowl, add additional bread if needed
- Take the boneless turkey breast length wise and split in half, but not all the way through
- Unfold the breast so the turkey opens like a book

- Salt and pepper turkey and lightly spread Dijon mustard all over
- Spread the stuffing evenly throughout the breast leaving a 1-inch border
- Starting from the short end of the breast roll tightly leaving the seam down
- Season the turkey roll all over with salt and pepper
- Wrap a cheesecloth all the way around and secure both ends with kitchen twine
- Also tie twine around the roast at least every 3 to 4 inches depending on the size of your breast, evenly spaced
- Brush room temperature butter evenly all over turkey and place on to a baking sheet
- Bake for about an hour and a half or until a thermometer inserted in the middle registers 155 degrees
- Remove from oven and tent with foil, let the turkey rest
- Remove twine and cheese cloth before cutting
- The internal temperature should reach 165 degrees

Slice Turkey and serve with Sage Mushroom Sauce.

Serves 4-6 people

Thai Salmon with Bangkok Curry Sauce

Ingredients

- 4 (8 ounce) fresh salmon fillets
- ½ cup fresh spinach julienne
- 1 whole lime cut into wedges
- Thai red chili sliced thin for garnish
- Serve rice and vegetables of your choice

Ingredients - Bangkok Curry Sauce

- 2 tablespoons vegetable oil
- 1 tablespoon red curry paste
- 1 can coconut milk
- ½ cup water
- 2 teaspoons fish sauce
- 2 teaspoons coconut sugar

Putting It All Together

- In a medium sauté pan combine the vegetable oil, curry paste and coconut milk
- Stir well until fragrant then add then the water, fish sauce, and coconut sugar
- Add the salmon fillet in the sauce and cook covered 2 to 3 minutes depending on the thickness of the fillets
- Just before salmon is done cooking sprinkle the spinach over the fillets and replace the cover and cook for another minute

Remove the salmon and serve on dinner plates with the sauce surrounding the fish and sprinkle lightly the red chilies and a side of lime wedge. Serve rice and vegetables of your choice.

Serves 4 people

Wrapped Salmon in Phyllo with Mornay Sauce

Ingredients

- 4 (6 ounce) salmon fillet deboned and skin removed
- 8 sheets of phyllo
- ½ cup melted butter
- 3 tablespoons Dijon mustard
- Salt and pepper to taste

Ingredients - Mornay Sauce

- 3 tablespoons butter
- 3 tablespoons flour
- 2 cups warm milk
- 2 ounces of grated gruyere cheese
- Pinch of nutmeg
- Salt and white pepper to taste

In medium saucepan melt butter and add the flour, cook until it thickens for about 1 minute. Whisk the two cups of milk in slowly until it is smooth and velvety. Add salt, pepper, nutmeg and the gruyere cheese. Simmer for a few minutes longer until everything is well incorporated, serve hot with the salmon. Set aside for service time with salmon.

Putting It All Together

- Preheat oven to 350 degrees
- Rub each fillet with mustard and sprinkle with salt and pepper
- Take two each of phyllo and brush each one with butter
- Place salmon on the edge of phyllo and fold over to make a complete wrap
- Repeat for the other fillets and brush the top of each wrapped salmon with melted butter
- Place into a baking pan and bake for 20 minutes or until golden brown

Serve on plates with Mornay sauce.

Serves 4 people

Desserts . . .

- ❖ *Almond Bourbon Honey Cake*
- ❖ *Apple Spice Cake with Cranberry Sauce*
- ❖ *Banana Foster Pecan Cream Brule*
- ❖ *Black Bottom Pie*
- ❖ *Chinese Five Spice Cake with Ginger Cream Anglaise Sauce*
- ❖ *Chocolate Pecan Pumpkin Rum Cake*
- ❖ *Coconut Almond Cream Cake*
- ❖ *Cranberry Almond Pudding with Almond Butter sauce*
- ❖ *Fudge Truffle Cheesecake*
- ❖ *Italian Cream Cake*
- ❖ *Key Lime Pie with Mango Cream Anglaise*
- ❖ *Lemon Blueberry Cake with Lemon Curd*
- ❖ *Mexican Chocolate Tart with Almond Cream Anglaise*
- ❖ *Meyer Lemon and Thyme Cream Brulée*
- ❖ *Mocha Cheesecake with Pecans*
- ❖ *No Bake Pumpkin Pecan Cheesecake*
- ❖ *Orange Carrot Cake with Grand Marnier Cream Cheese Frosting*
- ❖ *Oreo Mint Chocolate Jelly Roll with Cream de Menthe Sauce*
- ❖ *Pear Poached Pinot Noir Stuffed with Frangelico Mascarpone Cheese*
- ❖ *Pumpkin Oreo Pie Parfait*
- ❖ *Snick Doodle Cheesecake with Chocolate Sauce*
- ❖ *Sour Orange Pie*

Almond Bourbon Honey Cake

Ingredients

- 3 ¾ cup all-purpose flour
- 1 teaspoon baking powder
- 1 teaspoon soda
- 4 teaspoons cinnamon
- ½ teaspoon cloves
- ½ teaspoon allspice
- ½ teaspoon ginger
- 1 cup vegetable oil
- 1 cup honey
- 1 cup sugar
- ½ cup brown sugar
- 4 eggs
- 1 teaspoon almond extract
- 1 cup hot coffee
- ½ cup orange juice
- ¼ cup Kentucky bourbon
- ½ cup blanched almonds
- Cooking spray

Putting It All Together

- Preheat oven to 350 degrees
- Use cooking spray and flour (lightly dusted) to prepare Bundt cake pan
- In a large bowl whisk the flour, baking powder, baking soda and spices
- Make a well in the middle of bowl and add oil, honey, sugar, eggs, extract, coffee, orange juice, and bourbon
- Whisk with an electric mixer on low speed until well combined
- Spoon the mixture into the prepared Bundt cake pan and sprinkle almonds on top of batter
- Bake for 1 hour
- Remove the cake from the oven and check with a toothpick or knife by inserting into the middle of the cake. If it comes out clean it's done, if not continue to bake and check every five minutes.
- Let it cool for 10 minutes on wire rack and then invert it carefully from the pan back onto wire rack, best served warm

Serves 10-12 people

Apple Spice Cake with Cranberry Sauce

Ingredients - Cake

- 2 cups sugar
- 2 eggs at room temperature
- 1 ¼ cup vegetable oil
- 3 cups all-purpose flour
- 1 teaspoon baking soda
- 1 teaspoon cinnamon
- ½ teaspoon ginger
- ½ teaspoon clove
- ½ teaspoon allspice
- ½ teaspoon salt
- ¼ cup toasted and chopped walnuts
- 3 cups granny smith apples peeled and diced small
- 2 teaspoons vanilla extract
- ½ cup butterscotch morsels
- Cooking spray
- Powder sugar for atop cake

Putting It All Together

- With an electric mixer beat sugar and eggs, and then add the oil and vanilla and then beat until well incorporated
- In a separate bowl combine dry ingredients of flour, soda, spices, and salt until well mixed and then add to mixing bowl
- Add the diced apples and walnuts to the batter
- Pour into 2 eight-inch cake pans that have been prepared with cooking spray and lightly dusted with flour or lined with parchment paper
- Sprinkle butterscotch morsels on top
- Bake at 350 degrees for 1 hour
- Remove the cake from the oven and check with a toothpick or knife by inserting into the middle of the cake. If it comes out clean it's done, if not continue to bake and check every five minutes.
- Let the cake in the pans rest on wire rack for 15 minutes and when cool remove from the pans
- Sprinkle powder sugar atop the cake and serve with a side of cranberry sauce

Ingredients - Cranberry Sauce

- ½ cup sugar
- ½ cup orange juice
- 2 cups fresh cranberries
- 1 teaspoon lemon zest
- 1 tablespoon lemon juice
- 1 tablespoon of orange zest

Putting It All Together

- In a saucepan combine sugar and orange juice and bring to a boil
- Add cranberries, lemon zest and lemon juice,
- When cranberries start to pop lower heat and stir until they are soft in texture
- In a separate small bowl combine 2 tablespoons cold orange juice with 1 tablespoon cornstarch
- Mix well and stir into the cranberry sauce until it has thickened
- Remove from heat and cool
- Cover and refrigerate until serving time (when ready to serve, if sauce is too thick add additional orange juice for a smooth texture.)
- Upon serving time, put the cranberry sauce on the Apple Spice cake

Serves 10-12 people

Banana Foster Pecan Crème Brule

Ingredients - Custard

- 2 cups heavy cream
- ½ cup sugar
- 1 tablespoon vanilla extract
- 5 whole egg yolks
- 6 custard dishes (oven safe)

Putting It All Together

- Preheat oven to 275 degrees
- Combine cream, sugar, vanilla extract, and egg yolks into a bowl and mix well
- Place custard dishes in a deep baking pan with a half inch of water in pan
- Pour the custard into the 6 individual dishes evenly
- Bake 45 minutes to an hour or until custard jiggles slightly
- Remove pan from oven and using a pair of rubber tongs lift dishes out and place on a cooling rack for 30 minutes
- Cover and chill for at least 3 hours
- Prepare the topping below

Ingredients - Topping

- 3 tablespoons butter
- 3 tablespoons brown sugar
- 3 ripe bananas sliced
- 3 tablespoons roughly chopped pecans
- 6 teaspoons sugar
- 1 teaspoon vanilla extract

Putting It All Together

- Combine in a hot skillet, butter, brown sugar and the sliced bananas
- Cook on medium heat for 1 minute then douse with brandy for flame to ignite
- Once the brandy has extinguished, place the bananas on top of each custard
- Sprinkle each custard with chopped pecans 1 tablespoon of white sugar
- With a blow torch (or in an oven on high broil) brown the custards until the sugar has caramelized and serve immediately

Serves 6 people

Black Bottom Pie

Ingredients - Crust
- 24 Oreo cookies with cream inside
- 4 tablespoons melted butter

Putting It All Together
- Place cookies in the food processer and pulse until finely crumbled
- Add melted butter and mix well
- Place cookie mixture into a pie pan and press to form smoothly and evenly
- Bake at 350 degrees for 8 to 10 minutes
- Take out of the oven to cool on a wire rack

Ingredients - Filling
- 1/3 cup sugar
- 1/3 cup coco powder
- 2 tablespoons cornstarch
- Pinch of salt
- 1 ¼ cups white sugar
- 1 ¾ cups cream
- 2 tablespoons butter cut into small pieces
- 1 teaspoon vanilla extract
- 4 ounces dark chocolate chopped fine

Putting It All Together
- In a saucepan sift together sugar, coco powder, cornstarch and salt
- Gradually whisk in cream slowly cooking over medium heat stirring constantly
- Reduce heat and add the chocolate until it has thickened
- Remove from heat and whisk in the small pieces of butter and vanilla until well incorporated
- Pour the filling evenly into the prepared pie crust and refrigerate until set for approximately 2-3 hours

Ingredients - Topping
- 1 cup heavy cream
- ¼ cup powder sugar
- 1/8 teaspoon rum extract
- 1 bar of dark chocolate (shaved)
- 1 tablespoon coco powder (optional)

Putting It All Together
- In a cold mixing bowl add heavy cream and mix until the cream forms peaks
- Add powder sugar and rum to mixing bowl and mix until firm peaks are formed
- Spread the whip cream mixture evenly on top of the pie and garnish with chocolate shavings and/or sifted coco power on top

Serves 8 people

Chinese Five Spice Cake with Ginger Crème Anglaise Sauce

Ingredients - Cake

- 2 cups all-purpose flour
- 3 ½ teaspoons five spice powder
- ¼ teaspoon ground cinnamon
- 2 teaspoons baking soda
- ½ teaspoon salt
- 1 cup brown sugar
- ¾ cup white sugar
- 4 eggs at room temperature
- 1 ¼ cups vegetable oil
- 2 teaspoons vanilla extract
- 2 large Gala apples peeled and grated
- Powder sugar to sprinkle on top of cake
- Cooking spray

Putting It All Together

- Preheat oven to 350 degrees
- Spray the Bundt cake pan with cooking spray
- In a bowl whisk together the flour, five spice, cinnamon, baking soda and salt, and set aside
- In another bowl whisk together brown sugar, sugar and eggs until incorporated
- Add oil and vanilla to the bowl and whisk to combine
- Add the dry ingredients into the wet and using a spatula gently mix and fold the ingredients together until well combined
- Add the grated apple and fold into batter
- Pour the batter into the prepared Bundt cake pan and bake for 40 minutes
- Remove the cake from the oven and check with a toothpick or knife by inserting into the middle of the cake. If it comes out clean it's done, if not continue to bake and check every five minutes
- Let the cake cool on a wire rack for 10 minutes
- Remove the cake from the pan
- Using a sifter dust the top of cake with powder sugar
- Serve warm with Ginger Crème Anglaise

Ingredients - Ginger Crème Anglaise

- 1 cup of milk
- 6 egg yolks
- ½ cup sugar
- ½ teaspoon vanilla extract
- 1 tablespoon of fresh grated ginger or 1 teaspoon of ground ginger

Putting It All Together

- Scald the milk by bringing the temperature to lukewarm
- In a separate bowl mix in the egg yolks, sugar, and vanilla together until smooth
- Temper the warm milk into the egg yolk mixture slowly and cook over medium heat stirring constantly until thickened
- Add ginger into the mixture and stir well
- Strain the mixture and cover the sauce with a plastic wrap and refrigerate until ready to serve
- When ready to serve, top with heavy whipped cream and a side of the Ginger Crème Anglaise sauce
- **Serves 10-12 people**

Chocolate Pecan Pumpkin Rum Cake

Ingredients - Cake

- ½ cup toasted and chopped pecans
- 1 (15 ounce) can pureed pumpkin
- ½ cup coconut sugar or sugar
- ½ cup coconut oil
- 4 eggs at room temperature
- ¼ cup applesauce
- 1 box chocolate cake mix
- 1 ½ teaspoons ground cinnamon
- ½ teaspoon nutmeg
- 1/8 teaspoon ground cloves
- Cooking spray

Putting It All Together

- Preheat oven at 350 degrees
- Use cooking spray and flour to coat Bundt cake pan
- Sprinkle pecans on the bottom of the pan
- In a large bowl, beat pumpkin, sugar, oil, eggs, and applesauce until well blended
- In another bowl whisk cake mix and spices and gradually beat into pumpkin mixture
- Transfer the mixture to the prepared Bundt cake pan
- Bake for 55 minutes
- Remove the cake from the oven and check with a toothpick or knife by inserting into the middle of the cake. If it comes out clean it's done, if not continue to bake and check every five minutes.

Ingredients - Glaze

- 1 cup sugar
- ½ cup butter-cubed
- ¼ teaspoon ground cinnamon
- Pinch of ground cloves
- ½ cup Myers Dark Rum

Putting It All Together

- In a small saucepan combine sugar, butter, and spices and cook over medium heat until butter is melted
- Remove from heat, stir in the rum and cook for 3 minutes until sugar is dissolved
- Brush the glaze atop the warm cake evenly
- Serve warm

Serves 6-8 people

Coconut Almond Cream Cake

Ingredients - Cake

- 1 ¼ cups unsalted butter room temp
- 2 cups sugar
- 5 large eggs at room temp
- 1 ½ teaspoons vanilla extract
- ¼ teaspoon almond extract
- 3 cups cake flour
- 1 tablespoon baking powder
- ½ teaspoon salt
- 1 cup coconut milk
- 2 cups shredded sweet coconut
- 1/3 cup toasted sliced almonds
- ¼ cup toasted coconut

Putting It All Together

- Preheat oven to 350 degrees
- Grease three 8-inch baking pans lining each one with parchment paper
- In a large bowl with electric mixer beat the butter on medium speed for 4-5 min.
- Scrape the sides of bowl and then add sugar and mix for another 2 minutes
- Add eggs one at a time on low speed to combine, stir in the extracts
- In a smaller bowl combine cake flour, baking powder and salt, stir half of the dry ingredients into the cake batter
- Stir in the coconut milk and add the remaining dry ingredients until combined
- Stir in the shredded coconut
- Fill all three cake pans evenly with the batter and smooth the tops, and bake for about 30 minutes
- Remove the cake from the oven and check with a toothpick or knife by inserting into the middle of the cake. If it comes out clean it's done, if not continue to bake and check every five minutes.
- Allow the cake to cool on wire rack for 10 minutes at room temperature

Ingredients - Frosting

- 1 ½ cups unsalted butter room temperature
- 8 ounces cream cheese at room temperature
- ½ teaspoon almond extract
- ½ teaspoon vanilla extract
- ½ teaspoon salt
- 7 cups of powder sugar

Putting it All Together

- Beat the butter in a bowl with electric mixer until light and fluffy for 3 minutes
- Add cream cheese and beat for another minute or two until well combined
- Add the extracts and salt and then add in slowly the powder sugar and stir on low speed until well combined and then increasing the speed as needed to smooth the consistency
- Frost the top of first layer and then place next layer and frost the top and repeat final layer and frost the top and then spread frosting around the sides of cake
- Top of cake with toasted coconut and almonds

Serves 10-12 people

Cranberry Almond Pudding Cake

Ingredients - Cake

- 6 tablespoons butter
- 2 cups sugar
- 4 cups all-purpose flour
- 4 teaspoons baking powder
- 1 teaspoon salt
- 2 cups milk
- 1 (12 ounce) package cranberries
- ½ cup lightly brown chopped almonds
- Cooking spray

Putting It All Together

- Preheat oven to 325 degrees
- Use cooking spray and flour to prepare the Bundt pan
- Combine flour, baking powder and salt in a bowl and set aside
- In another bowl cream together 6 tablespoon butter and 2 cups sugar until light and fluffy
- Beat in the flour mixture alternately with milk and stir in cranberries and almonds
- Pour batter into the Bundt pan and bake for about 50 to 60 minutes
- Remove the cake from the oven and check with a toothpick or knife by inserting into the middle of the cake. If it comes out clean it's done, if not continue to bake and check every five minutes.
- Invert cake on wire rack to cool

Ingredients - Hot Butter Sauce

- 1 cup butter
- 1 cup heavy cream
- 2 cups sugar
- 1 teaspoon almond extract

Putting It All Together

- In a saucepan combine, sugar, butter, and cream
- Bring to boil over medium heat and reduce heat and let simmer for 10 minutes
- Remove from heat and add the almond extract
- Drizzle sauce over cake and serve

Serves 4-6 people

Fudge Truffle Cheesecake

Ingredients - Chocolate Crumb Crust

- 1 ½ cups crushed vanilla wafer cookies
- ½ cup powder sugar
- 1/3 cup Hershey coco
- 1/3 cup melted butter

Putting It All Together

- In a medium bowl combine the above ingredients and mix well
- Press the mixture firmly and evenly in spring form pan and set aside

Ingredients - Filling

- 2 cups of Hershey's semi-sweet chocolate chips.
- 3 (8 ounce) cream cheese at room temperature
- 1 (14 ounce) can sweetened condensed milk
- 4 eggs at room temperature
- 2 teaspoons vanilla extract

Putting It All Together

- Heat oven to 300 degrees
- In a heavy saucepan over very low heat melt chocolate chips stirring constantly and set aside
- Using an electric mixing bowl add the cream cheese and mix until fluffy while scraping the sides of the bowl gradually
- Add the condensed milk until smooth
- Add melted chocolate chips and the eggs and vanilla and mix well until all is incorporated
- Pour batter into the prepared chocolate crumb crust pan and bake for 1 hour
- Remove the cake from the oven and check with a toothpick or knife by inserting into the middle of the cake. If it comes out clean it's done, if not continue to bake and check every five minutes.
- Cool on a wire rack and refrigerate for 2-3 hours or overnight before serving

Serves 10 to 12 people

Italian Cream Cake

Ingredients - Cake

- 1 cup buttermilk
- 1 teaspoon baking soda
- ½ cup butter
- ½ cup shortening
- 2 cups white sugar
- 5 eggs at room temperature
- 1 teaspoon vanilla extract
- 1 cup flaked coconut
- 1 teaspoon baking powder
- 2 cups all-purpose flour
- Cooking spray

Putting It All Together

- Preheat the oven to 350 degrees
- Prepare 3 nine-inch round pans with cooking spray and flour or line each one with parchment paper
- In a small bowl dissolve baking soda and buttermilk and set aside
- In a large bowl cream together with an electric mixer butter, shortening, and sugar until light and fluffy while scraping down sides to incorporate all
- Add in the eggs, buttermilk mixture, vanilla, coconut, baking powder and flour to the bowl and stir until combined
- Pour batter evenly into all three pans
- Bake for 30 to 35 minutes
- Remove the cake from the oven and check with a toothpick or knife by inserting into the middle of the cake. If it comes out clean it's done, if not continue to bake and check every five minutes.
- Cool on a wire rack for 10 minutes before taking out of the pan

Ingredients - Frosting

- 8 ounces cream cheese
- ½ cup butter at room temperature
- 1 teaspoon vanilla extract
- 4 cups powder sugar
- 2 tablespoons cream
- ½ cup chopped walnuts
- 1 cup lightly toasted shredded coconut

Putting It All Together

- In medium bowl combine cream cheese, butter, vanilla, and powder sugar
- Beat until light and fluffy
- Stir in walnuts and shredded coconut
- Frost the cake on all three layers top and sides and serve

Serves 12 to 14 people

Key Lime Pie with Mango Crème Anglaise

Ingredients - Crust

- 1 cup finely crushed graham crackers
- 3 tablespoons melted butter

Putting It All Together

- Preheat oven to 350 degrees
- In a medium bowl combine the above ingredients and mix well
- Combine graham crackers and melted butter mix well and press onto a pie pan evenly, bake crust for 10 minutes, take out of oven to cool and set aside.

Ingredients - Filling

- 3 cups sweetened condensed milk
- ½ cup sour cream
- ¾ cup Trader Joe's key lime juice
- 1 fresh lime
- 1 tablespoon key lime zest

Putting It All Together

- In a medium bowl using an electric mixer combine the condensed milk, sour cream, lime juice and zest from one lime
- Mix well and pour into prepared pie pan
- Bake the key lime pie for about 10 - 15 minutes or until center of pie jiggles a bit
- Take the pie out to cool and then refrigerate for 2-3 hours
- When ready to serve, top with heavy whipped cream, slices of lime and a side of the Mango Crème Anglaise sauce

Ingredients - Mango Crème Anglaise Sauce

- 1 cup of milk
- 6 egg yolks
- ½ cup sugar
- ½ teaspoon vanilla extract
- ½ cup mango puree

Putting It All Together

- Scald the milk by bringing the temperature to lukewarm
- In a separate bowl mix in the egg yolks, sugar, and vanilla together until smooth
- Temper the warm milk into the egg yolk mixture slowly and cook over medium heat stirring constantly until it has thickened a bit
- Add the mango puree into the mixture and stir well
- Strain the mixture and cover the sauce with a plastic wrap and refrigerate until ready to serve
- When ready to serve, top with heavy whipped cream, slices of lime and a side of the Mango Crème Anglaise sauce

Serves 10 to 12 people

Lemon Blueberry Cake with Lemon Curd

Ingredients

- 2 large eggs at room temperature
- 1 cup granulated sugar
- 1 cup sour cream
- ½ cup vegetable oil
- 1 teaspoon vanilla extract
- ¼ teaspoon salt
- 2 cups all-purpose flour
- 2 teaspoons baking powder
- 1 teaspoon lemon zest
- 1 tablespoon fresh lemon juice
- ½ tablespoon cornstarch
- 2 cups fresh blueberries
- 1 (8 ounce) Jar of lemon Curd
- Cooking spray

Putting It All Together

- Preheat oven at 375 degrees
- Lightly spray a spring form pan and with parchment paper on the bottom of the pan
- Beat 2 eggs and sugar with a whisk attachment on high speed for 5 minutes until light in color and thick
- Add 1 cup sour cream, ½ cup oil, vanilla, salt, and whisk on low speed until well combined
- In another bowl whisk the flour and baking soda, then add it to the batter 1/3 at a time (do not over mix)
- Add lemon juice and zest.
- Rinse the blueberries and drain well
- Toss the blueberries in cornstarch and lemon juice stirring until well combined
- Pour half of the batter into pan and pour half of the blueberries on top of the batter spreading evenly
- Top the rest of batter with the blueberries
- Bake at 375 degrees for 45 minutes
- Remove the cake from the oven and check with a toothpick or knife by inserting into the middle of the cake. If it comes out clean it's done, if not continue to bake and check every five minutes.
- Cool cake on wire rack for 10 minutes
- Remove cake from pan
- Serve with warmed Lemon Curd on the side

Serves 10 to 14 people

Mexican Chocolate Tart with Almond Crème Anglaise

Ingredients - Nut Mixture

- 1 large egg white
- 2 tablespoons sugar
- 1 tablespoon brown sugar
- 1 teaspoon ground cinnamon
- ¼ teaspoon salt
- 1/8 teaspoon cayenne pepper
- 1 ½ cups of pecans chopped
- Cooking spray

Putting it All Together

- Preheat oven to 350 degrees
- Spray the baking sheet with cooking spray
- Whisk all the ingredients except the pecans in a medium bowl
- Stir in pecans and spread the mixture onto the baking sheet
- Bake until browned and dry for about 30 minutes
- Remove from oven and cool down
- Separate nuts and remove excess coating (this all can be done ahead of time and stored in airtight container at room temperature)

Ingredients - Crust

- 1 cup chocolate wafer cookies crushed fine
- ¼ cup sugar
- ½ teaspoon ground cinnamon
- 1/8 teaspoon salt
- 5 tablespoons melted butter

Putting it All Together

- Preheat oven at 350 degrees
- Pulse the chocolate wafer cookies, sugar, cinnamon and salt in a food processor until combined
- Add melted butter to the food processor and blend until well combined
- Press the crumb mixture evenly into a 9-inch tart pan and bake for 20 minutes
- Remove from oven and cool on a wire rack

Ingredients - Filling

- 1 cup heavy cream
- 4 ounces semi-sweet chocolate
- 1 (3.1 ounce) disc Mexican Chocolate chopped
- ½ stick unsalted butter, cut into 4 pieces, room temperature
- 2 teaspoons vanilla extract
- 1 teaspoon ground cinnamon
- ¼ teaspoon salt
- Whip cream for topping

Putting It All Together

- Bring heavy cream to simmer in a saucepan
- Remove from heat and add chocolate and whisk until melted
- Add butter 1 piece at a time and whisk until smooth
- Combine the vanilla, cinnamon, and salt to mixture
- Pour filling into the prepared tart pan and chill in the refrigerator for 20 minutes
- Add the pecans in a circle around the top of tart
- Chill over night
- Serve with a dollop of whip cream and a side of Almond Crème Anglaise

Ingredients - Almond Crème Anglaise Sauce

- ½ cup whole milk
- ½ cup heavy cream
- ½ teaspoon almond extract
- 3 large egg yolks
- 3 tablespoons sugar

Putting It All Together

- Combine milk and heavy cream and extract in a saucepan
- Bring mixture to simmer and remove from heat to keep warm
- Whisk egg yolks and sugar in a medium bowl to blend
- Gradually whisk the warm cream mixture with the egg yolk slowly and return back into the saucepan
- Stir over low heat until the custard thickens for about 5 minutes
- Pour the sauce through a strainer into a clean bowl
- Cool and refrigerate when ready to serve

Serves 12 people

Meyer Lemon and Thyme Crème Brulée

Ingredients - Custard

- 2 cups heavy cream
- 6 tablespoons of sugar divided
- 4 large egg yolks
- 2 Meyer lemons- zested
- Juice of half of Meyer lemon
- ½ teaspoon vanilla extract
- Pinch of kosher salt
- ½ teaspoon chopped fresh thyme
- 4 - 5-ounce custard dishes

Putting It All Together

- Preheat oven to 300 degrees
- In a small saucepan heat the cream and half of the sugar over medium heat do not bring to a boil but low simmer for 6 to 8 minutes
- Meanwhile whisk egg yolks sugar, vanilla, Meyer lemon juice, zest, salt, and thyme together until combined
- Gradually ladle the hot cream into the egg mixture while continuing to whisk until smooth
- Pour mixture through a fine strainer
- Evenly fill 4 (5-ounce) dishes with the custard
- Place in a deep baking dish and pour hot water halfway up the sides of the dishes
- Bake for 30 to 40 minutes until custards are set
- Carefully remove dishes with rubber tongs to a cooling rack for 30 minutes
- Cover and chill for at least 3 hours or up to 3 days before serving
- Sprinkle each custard with 1 tablespoon of white sugar
- With a blow torch (or in an oven on high broil) brown the custards until the sugar has caramelized and serve immediately

Serves 4-6people

Mocha Cheesecake with Pecans

Ingredients - Crust

- 1 ½ cups crushed vanilla wafers
- 4 tablespoons butter melted

Putting It All Together

- Preheat oven at 350 degrees
- Coat a spring form pan with cooking spray
- In a bowl combine crushed vanilla wafers and butter
- Press the mixture evenly on the bottom of spring form pan
- Bake for 10-15 minutes and cool on wire rack and set aside

Ingredients - Filling

- 1 cup white sugar
- 4 ounces cream cheese at room temperature
- 2 large eggs at room temperature
- 8 ounces bittersweet chocolate
- 2 tablespoons heavy cream
- 1 cup sour cream
- 1 ½ tablespoons instant espresso powder
- ½ cup hot water
- 1 teaspoon vanilla extract
- ¾ cup chopped pecans
- Topping: Whip cream and/or raspberries (optional)

Putting it All Together

- In a large bowl combine cream cheese and sugar and beat with electric mixer until smooth
- Add the eggs one at a time until well blended but do not over beat
- Melt chocolate in a DBL boiler until well melted and smooth
- Cool the chocolate at room temperature before adding into the cheesecake batter
- Combine well the heavy cream and sour cream and stir into the mixture
- Dissolve the espresso in the ½ cup of hot water and cool to room temperature
- Add the cooled espresso to the batter along with the vanilla while scraping the inside of bowl to incorporate
- Pour the mixture into the prepared pan
- Top with the pecans and bake for 45 minutes until the center will be slightly jiggly (it will firm as the cheesecake cools down on a rack)
- 20 minutes or halfway through the cooking process place foil on top of cheesecake to prevent the pecans from burning
- Remove the cheesecake from the oven and cool on a wire rack
- Refrigerate at least 3-4 hours or overnight prior to serving
- Prior to serving, use a sharp knife along the inside edges of the cheesecake pan and then carefully release the latch on the outside pan and lift the cheesecake out
- Serve with a dollop of fresh whip cream or raspberries - **Serves 10 to 12 people**

No Bake Pumpkin Pecan Cheesecake

Ingredients - Crust

- 1 ½ cups finely crushed graham crackers
- ½ cup melted butter

Putting It All Together

- Combine graham crackers and melted butter and mix well,
- Press into an 8-inch spring form pan evenly and refrigerate

Ingredients - Filling

- 1 cup heavy cream
- 2 (8 ounce) cream cheese softened
- 1 (15 ounce) can pumpkin puree
- 1 cup powder sugar
- 1 teaspoon vanilla extract
- 1 teaspoon cinnamon
- ½ teaspoon nutmeg
- ¼ teaspoon salt
- Topping: Whip Cream and ½ cup chopped pecans (toasted)

Putting It All Together

- In a bowl beat heavy cream to stiff peaks and set aside
- In another bowl attached to an electric mixer beat cream cheese until light and fluffy
- Add pumpkin puree until smooth
- Add powder sugar, vanilla, extract, cinnamon, nutmeg, and salt mix until all is incorporated
- Fold the whip cream into the pumpkin mixture until well incorporated
- Pour into the prepared crust
- Top the cheesecake with toasted pecans and whip cream around the border of cheesecake

Serves 8 to 10 people

Orange Carrot Cake with Grand Marnier Cream Cheese Frosting

Ingredients - Orange Carrot Cake

- 2 cups toasted chopped walnuts
- 2 ½ cups all-purpose flour
- 2 teaspoons soda
- 2 teaspoons nutmeg and cinnamon
- ¼ teaspoon salt
- 1 ½ cups unsalted butter softened
- 2 ½ cups sugar
- ¼ cup milk
- Zest of 1 orange
- ¼ cup orange juice
- 1 ½ teaspoons vanilla extract
- 2 cups grated carrots
- Cooking spray

Putting It All Together

- Preheat oven to 375 degrees
- Spray or line 2 - 9-inch round cake pans with parchment paper and set aside
- Combine the dry ingredients together in a separate bowl
- Cream butter and sugar in a large bowl with an electric mixer on medium speed - reduce speed and blend eggs one at a time while adding milk gradually alternating with flour and milk (dry ingredients) until the batter is smooth
- Stir in orange zest, juice, extract, carrots and chopped walnuts
- Divide mixture into the two pans and bake for 40 minutes
- Remove cake from oven and check with a toothpick or knife by inserting into the middle. If it comes out clean it's done, if not bake and check every five minutes.
- Cool pans on a wire rack for 10-15 minutes prior to frosting

Ingredients - Frosting

- ½ cup unsalted butter cut into 2 tablespoon size pieces
- 2 (8 ounce) cream cheeses
- 4 cups powder sugar
- 1 teaspoon vanilla extract
- 1 tablespoon orange liqueur
- 2 tablespoons orange zest

Putting It All Together

- Mix the butter and cream cheese until well blended and smooth
- Add powder sugar, extract, orange liqueur and orange zest and mix well
- Spread cream cheese frosting on both layers of cake and sides
- Sprinkle additional walnuts on top if desired

Serves 10 to 12 people

Oreo Mint Chocolate Jelly Roll with Crème de Menth Sauce

Ingredients - Cake

- 3 Eggs room temperature
- ¾ cup sugar
- 2 teaspoons brewed coffee
- 1 teaspoon vanilla extract
- ¼ cup coco powder
- Powder Sugar
- ¼ teaspoon salt
- 1 teaspoon baking powder
- ¾ cup all-purpose flour
- Cooking spray

Putting It All Together

- Preheat oven to 350 degrees
- Line a sheet pan 10X15 with foil and spray with cooking spray
- Beat the eggs at high speed for 3 minutes until frothy
- Beat in sugar, coffee, and extract
- Whisk together coco, salt, baking powder and flour
- Stir into the wet ingredients until blended
- Spread the batter evenly into the pan with spatula and bake in oven for 9 to 10 minutes
- While cake is baking, set a large clean dish towel on countertop and dust with powder sugar
- Remove cake from the oven and flip onto the towel sprinkled with powder sugar
- Working horizontally, fold the edge of the towel over the cake to roll the cake tightly into a long roll
- Leave wrapped for at least thirty minutes

Ingredients - Crème De Menthe Filling

- 1 cup of heavy cream
- 4 tablespoons powder sugar
- 1 tablespoon crème de menthe
- 1 to 2 drops green food coloring
- ½ cup chocolate Oreo cookies (crushed)

Putting It All Together

- Beat the heavy cream in a bowl with an electric mixer fitted with the whisk attachment
- Slowly add in the powder sugar, crème de menthe extract, food coloring and crushed cookies until stiff peaks are achieved
- Set aside in the refrigerator

Ingredients - Frosting

- 2 cups milk chocolate chips
- 1 ¼ cup heavy cream
- ½ teaspoon vanilla extract
- ¼ cup mini chocolate chips

Putting it All Together

- Place chocolate chips in medium bowl
- Heat the cream in a small saucepan over low heat until the cream starts to bubble around the edges
- Pour the cream over chocolate chips and let it set for 30 seconds
- Whisk until smooth and add vanilla extract
- Stir until smooth and then refrigerate for one hour to thicken

Ingredients - Crème de Menthe Sauce

- 1 cup milk
- 6 egg yolks
- ½ cup sugar
- 1 to 2 tablespoons crème de menthe to your taste

Putting it All Together

- Scald milk and set aside
- Mix egg yolks and sugar together until smooth
- Slowly add the hot milk into the egg yolk mixture
- Cook over medium heat in a saucepan until it has thickened for about 5 minutes
- Remove from the stove and cool
- When fully cooled add 1-2 tablespoons crème de menthe to taste

To Assemble Chocolate Jelly Roll

- Retrieve the cake roll from the refrigerator
- Carefully unroll the cake roll from the dish towel
- Spread the filling evenly across the cake leaving a one-inch border all around
- Use the dish towel again -- roll the cake back into a roll
- Refrigerate for at least one hour before spreading the frosting on the jelly roll
- Retrieve the cake and place the cake carefully on a rectangular platter or pan
- Frost the cake evenly on all sides
- Garnish with crumbled chocolate crème de menthe Oreo cookies
- Slice when ready and serve with a side of Crème de menthe sauce

Serves 10 to 12 people

Pear Poached in Pinot Noir Stuffed with Frangelico Mascarpone Cheese

Ingredients – Poached Pear

- 1 bottle Pinot Noir
- 4 teaspoons black peppercorns
- 1 vanilla bean split in half and scraped
- 2 tablespoons orange zest
- 6 cardamom pods
- 1 ½ cups white sugar
- 6 ripe pears peeled, leave stem on

Ingredients - Frangelico Pecan and Mascarpone filling

- ½ cup mascarpone cheese
- ¼ cup finely chopped pecans
- 2 tablespoons Frangelico liquor

Mix all ingredients together

Putting It All Together

- Place the wine, peppercorns, vanilla bean paste, orange zest, cardamom and sugar in 2-quart saucepan
- Stir on medium heat until sugar has dissolved
- Bring the sauce to a boil and then turn down the heat and place pears in the liquid and continue to cook for 30 to 45 minutes
- Remove pears and set aside to cool
- Strain the solids in poaching liquid and discard
- Return the liquid back into the saucepan and reduce until thick for about 5 to 10 minutes
- When pears are cool, use a melon baller and remove the inner core of pear and stuff each pear with the mascarpone filling
- Serve with the reduction of Pinot Noir Sauce

Serves 6 people

Pumpkin Oreo Pie Parfait

Ingredients

- 1 package (3.5 ounce) vanilla pudding mix
- 2 cups cold milk
- 1 can (15 ounce) purred pumpkin
- ½ teaspoon cinnamon
- ¼ teaspoon nutmeg
- 1/8 teaspoon ground clove
- 1 cup crushed Oreo cookies
- 1 cup heavy cream whipped to firm peaks
- 6 slender parfait glasses

Putting It All Together

- In a large bowl whip the vanilla pudding and milk together and let set for 5 minutes
- Add and stir in the pumpkin and spices
- Using the parfait glasses, you will now make equal layers starting with a small amount of crumble cookies and then pumpkin/pudding mix and repeat for each layer until you have filled all the parfait glasses
- Top each glass with an Oreo cookie and dollop of whip cream

Serves 6 people

Snickerdoodle Cheesecake with Chocolate Sauce

Ingredients - Crust

- 1 ½ cups of shortbread cookie crumbs
- 3 tablespoons melted butter
- 1 teaspoon ground cinnamon
- Cooking spray

Putting It All Together

- Preheat oven to 350 degrees
- Use cooking spray to coat an 8" spring form pan
- In a large bowl, combine shortbread cookie crumbs and butter and mix until all is incorporated
- Press the mixture into the bottom of pan evenly and set aside in the refrigerator

Ingredients - Filling

- 3 (8 ounce) cream cheese
- 1 cup white sugar
- ¼ cup sour cream
- 3 large eggs at room temperature
- 2 teaspoons vanilla extract
- ¼ teaspoon ground cinnamon
- Pinch of salt
- Package of Snickerdoodle cookies for garnish

Putting It All Together

- In a medium bowl, use an electric mixer to beat the cream cheese until smooth and scrape down the sides of the bowl while mixing
- Add the sugar and sour cream and beat until light and fluffy, again scraping down the sides while mixing
- Add eggs one at a time beating well between each addition
- Add the vanilla, cinnamon and salt and continue mixing
- Retrieve the cookie crust from the refrigerator
- Pour the smooth batter over the cookie dough crust and bake for 1 hour until slightly jiggly in the center
- Turn the oven off and open the door slightly to let the cheesecake cool for about 1 hour
- Refrigerate overnight
- Prior to serving, garnish the cake with whip cream, snickerdoodle cookies and the chocolate sauce

Serves 10 to 12 people

Sour Orange Pie

Ingredients - Crust

- 2 cups vanilla wafers crushed fine
- 3 tablespoons sugar
- 6 tablespoons unsalted butter melted

Putting It All Together

- Preheat oven to 350 degrees
- In a large bowl, combine vanilla wafers, sugar and melted butter and mix until all is incorporated
- Press the mixture into the bottom of a pie pan evenly and bake in the middle of the rack for 10 to 15 minutes
- Remove from oven and cool
- Reduce the oven heat to 325 degrees and make the filling

Ingredients – Filling

- 5 large egg yolks
- 1 (14 ounce) can sweetened condensed whole milk
- 2 tablespoons heavy cream
- ½ cup sour orange juice, or use 1 part each grapefruit juice, lemon juice and orange juice
- 2 tablespoons sour orange zest or 1 tablespoon each orange and lemon zest
- Whip cream to serve atop pie

Putting It All Together

- Beat egg yolks well until they have lightened in color for about 1 minute
- Add condensed milk and two tablespoons of heavy cream and stir well
- Add sour orange juice and zest and stir to make sure everything is well incorporated
- Pour the filling into the crust and bake in the middle of the rack for about 15 minutes
- Remove the pie from the oven and let it rest on a wire rack until cool
- Once cooled, refrigerate the pie until it is firm and then garnish with whip cream prior to serving

Serves 6 to 8 people

CPSIA information can be obtained
at www.ICGtesting.com
Printed in the USA
JSHW041829030323
38413JS00002BA/32

9 781977 2581